Hope In Suffering

Devotions to Help You Through Hardship

Revised edition

Evelyn Bray

Light Hill Publishing

Connect with Evelyn on Facebook at
www.facebook.com/evelynbray.author
Or follow her blog at https://evelynbray-lighthill.blogspot.com

"Scripture quotations taken from the New American Standard Bible®, Copyright © 1960, 1962, 1963, 1968, 1971, 1972, 1973, 1975, 1977, 1995 by The Lockman Foundation
Used by permission." (www.Lockman.org)

ISBN-10: 0-692-79354-2
ISBN-13: 978-0-692-79354-1

Copyright © 2016 by Evelyn Bray, First Edition
Second printing © 2022 by Evelyn Bray, Revised Edition

All rights reserved. No part of this book may be reproduced in any manner without written permission except in the case of brief quotations included in critical articles and reviews. For information, please contact the author.

Image from Bigstock.com

Cover design by Evelyn Bray

To: My Twins
Without you this would never have come about.
I long for the day when I can finally hold you.

Table of contents

Waiting on God	6
God's Comfort in Suffering	9
God's Sovereignty over Suffering	43
Our Response to Suffering	79
Stories of Suffering	115
Hope in Suffering	136
Appendix A: Is Faith Enough?	138
Appendix B: Why is There Suffering?	142
Notes	149

Waiting on God

I come again to kneel at the throne
Pleading for my prayers to be heard
Waiting for a hand from the Almighty
Hoping that my urgency is understood

Disappointment creeps into my heart
As silence meets my request once more
Clinging to hope I appeal yet again
Hoping that this time I won't be looked over

Hope is weak when disappointment abounds
Trust breaks all the more easily
And faith loses its grasp
As doubt piles on readily

My heart cries "Where are You?
Why have You not heard me?"
As tears rush in to obstruct all sight
And evict what's left of peace

"How long must I wait? What must I do?"
The pleas pour in as if more words
Will increase my chances of being heard
As the persistent knocker on a door of wood

Where do I turn when the All-Faithful answers not?
What comfort is there to be found without the Comforter?
Can I have peace without the Peacemaker?
Who do I hope in if not the Father?

Can I be content to wait for His timing?
To trust that I am heard when met with doubt?
To be persistent in hope and yet peaceful
With no surety that it will turn out?

Where does my hope rest or surety lie?
In what is my strength and peace

My life in all its measure
My soul when my breaths cease?

Can I be content to wait
On the One who never fails,
To never lose faith
In the midst of life's gales?

I come with the hurt in my heart
To be healed by the great El Ohim
And trust Him to right the wrongs
And give me peace in the mean time.

Evelyn Bray

God's Comfort in Suffering

"God, like a father, doesn't just give advice. He gives Himself. He becomes the husband to the grieving widow (Isaiah 54:5). He becomes the comforter to the barren woman (Isaiah 54:1). He becomes the father of the orphaned (Psalm 10:14). He becomes the bridegroom of the single person (Isaiah 62:5). He is the healer to the sick (Exodus 15:26). He is the wonderful counselor to the confused and depressed (Isaiah 9:6)."

Joni Erickson Tada[i]

Therefore, there is now no condemnation for those who are in Christ Jesus.
Romans 8:1

~

If you believe that Jesus is the Son of God (and is God Himself), that He was born of a virgin, crucified, resurrected and ascended into heaven, and that belief produces fruit in your life and a love for God and His righteousness, then you are "in Christ". You are saved from sin and death, and justified before God. Whatever you have done has been forgiven and cast away. It does not define you any longer. When God looks at you, He sees His Son, holy and blameless. This is your identity now. You have free access to God and an inheritance and future with Him as an heir with Christ. He will not condemn you for what you have already repented of, and will not change His mind about how He sees you or treats you. You are secure in Him.

And He has said to me "My grace is sufficient for you, for power is perfected in weakness." Most gladly, therefore, I will rather boast about my weaknesses, so that the power of Christ may dwell in me.
2 Corinthians 12:9

~

Paul had been talking about a "thorn in his flesh" that he had asked God to take away. Rather than taking it away, or giving Paul some reprieve from his suffering, God merely said "My grace is sufficient for you." God had given him (or allowed him to have) that thorn to keep him humble, to keep him from having a reason to boast about himself, and to remind him that he was a human formed from the same sin-filled clay as every other person. At the end of the day we are all still sinful humans that would be lost in the deepest mire if it were not for the saving grace of God alone. It is His grace that pulls us from our lost state and gives us an inheritance with Him. It is His grace that paid the debt for our sins and gave us freedom from bondage to sin. It is His grace that gave us faith and the foundation to become like Him; in the end, perfected. His grace has given us everything we need to survive and more than we could ever hope for. It is sufficient and then some. But His grace is not always evident when life is easy, when we don't feel the need for sustenance. We are so often tempted to say "I did this good thing" or "I can handle this on my own," and forget that it is really God behind us and before us. Sometimes we need a thorn to remind us that we are nothing without God. It takes something painful to humble us, to bring our heads down out of the clouds and see where and what we truly are. Then we can see that it is His power driving us. It is through our weakness, when we do not feel capable, that God's power is revealed. May we ever be in that state of total dependence on His grace.

My soul waits in silence for God only, from Him is my salvation. He only is my rock and my salvation, my stronghold; I shall not be greatly shaken.
Psalm 62:1-2

~

Belief in Christ is the only way we can be free from the bondage of sin and its consequences and go to heaven. There is no other door, channel or outlet. His death on the cross is the only payment acceptable for the debt of our sins. We can only become "good enough" through His righteousness; nothing of ourselves can do it. He is mightier than all. He cannot be conquered, changed or moved. There is none that can defeat Him. Therefore He is the safest rock to build on, the most stable foundation to cling to, and the mightiest stronghold in which to take refuge. When we are safe in Him, danger can only get as close as we let it. We have to take ourselves inside the fortress and cling to the rock to be safe. God has promised to protect, provide for and save us. Trust in that and wait patiently for the storm to pass.

> *Blessed be the God and Father of our Lord Jesus Christ, the Father of mercies and God of all comfort, who comforts us in our affliction so that we will be able to comfort those who are in any affliction with the comfort with which we ourselves are comforted by God.*
> *2 Corinthians 1:3-4*

~

God is the Creator and Father of every good thing. He had mercy on us even when we were enemies with Him because of our sin. He is also the father of comfort. His name is love. He is the epitome of love, kindness, gentleness, etc. and He embodies those things completely and perfectly. He cannot be mean, cruel or even indifferent. He can only be loving toward us, so when we come to Him with our pain and sorrow, He will comfort us with His love and peace. He is our only true source of consolation, the only One that can give us true peace. And He gives us comfort to the extent that we will be able to give it to others. His love benefits us most when we share it.

> *The LORD is near to the brokenhearted and saves those who are crushed in spirit. Many are the afflictions of the righteous, but the LORD delivers him out of them all.*
> *Psalm 34:18-19*

~

Has your heart been broken? Are you full of grief and sorrow? Do you feel crushed, as if you were under a heavy weight from which you can't get away? Do you have so many bad things happening right now that you feel overwhelmed and you just can't keep your head above water? God is there. He is with you. You may feel alone, abandoned, shipwrecked, but you are never alone. God is there to save you. He is there to heal your heart; to remove the burden, to rescue you from your torment. He loves you. Turn to Him. Run to His shelter. Give Him your burdens and broken heart and let Him carry the load. Let Him heal you. Rest in His comforting arms.

> *Before I formed you in the womb I knew you, and before you were born I consecrated you.*
> *Jeremiah 1:5a*

~

This verse talks about the calling of the prophet Jeremiah, but the idea applies to everyone. God knew each of us before we were born. He knew what we would look like and what we would do, what would become of us and what would happen to us. He planned our physical form and our personality. The Bible also says that God made everything beautiful in its time. You may think that you are not beautiful, that maybe God doesn't care about your appearance. Believing that you are ugly is calling God a liar and a bad craftsman, which is a dangerous and untrue thing to say. God says you are beautiful because you are His child. You are precious to Him. He made you with His hands. Dwell on that for a minute.

He also knows all of your life's events. It doesn't mean that He planned for bad things to happen, but He did know that they would. We live in a fallen world where people sin. There is suffering because of sin (the direct consequences of something someone did), but also because we are born in sin. Original sin is the idea that we are imperfect people because the first people sinned, and that "curse" has fallen to every human in history, and also to nature. It is a part of how the world functions. But don't think that because God allows it that He doesn't care. He does care. That is why He sent His only Son as a sacrifice in your place so that you could be with Him in the future. One day you can leave this broken world and broken body behind to spend eternity with Christ in perfection. The suffering here will only last for a little while, but you have forever to look forward to. So put your hope and trust in the One who made you, Who cares for you more than any other, Who made the ultimate sacrifice for you to be with Him for eternity. Turn to Him for the strength to get through this life until you can be with Him. Trust the One who knows what will happen in your future, the only One that can make it work out for good.

> *In all their affliction He was afflicted, and the angel of His presence saved them; in His love and in His mercy He redeemed them, and He lifted them and carried them all the days of old.*
> *Isaiah 63:9*

~

Remember the Israelites, how they were in captivity and God freed them? Yet they continually turned from Him to other gods. Through it all God never forsook them. You are no less to Him than they were. Look at what He says about you. In your afflictions, He is afflicted. He feels what you are going through. He doesn't turn away so that He won't see it. He is right there experiencing it with you. And the angel of His presence will save you. His presence is the greatest joy, comfort and peace that you could ever have. It won't make the bad things go away, but it will comfort you and help you to endure them. Focus on His presence rather than your pain. He will deliver you. He will redeem you with His love and mercy. He will lift and carry you all the days of your life. Will you let Him?

For You formed my inward parts; You wove me in my mother's womb. I will give thanks to You, for I am fearfully and wonderfully made; wonderful are Your works, and my soul knows it very well. My frame was not hidden from You, when I was made in secret, and skillfully wrought in the depths of the earth; Your eyes have seen my unformed substance; and in Your book were all written the days that were ordained for me, when as yet there was not one of them.
Psalm 139:13-16

~

God created you. He personally designed you to be as you are, with His own hands—before you were born. He planned out your whole life before you were even conceived. He knows you better than you know yourself. And He loves you. You are His child, His creation. He cherishes you and knows you intimately. Go to Him. Accept His love. Trust Him, He knows what you are going through and will take care of you. Thank Him for His love and care, but also for making you as you are. He made you that way for a purpose and He delights in you.

Then you will say on that day, "I will give thanks to You, O Lord; for although You were angry with me, Your anger is turned away, and You comfort me. Behold, God is my salvation, I will trust and not be afraid; for the Lord God is my strength and song, and He has become my salvation." Therefore you will joyously draw water from the springs of salvation. And in that day you will say, "Give thanks to the Lord, call on His name. Make known His deeds among the peoples; make them remember that His name is exalted." Praise the Lord in song, for He has done excellent things; let this be known throughout the earth. Cry aloud and shout for joy, O inhabitant of Zion, for great in your midst is the Holy One of Israel.
Isaiah 12

~

God is everything good. He is our salvation, refuge, comfort, strength and joy. He has given us every blessing and good thing we have. He can and will give us more than everything we need to survive. He created us with a purpose. He is the One we can give our fears and sorrows to in return for His for strength, comfort and guidance. He should be our everything. See all that He has done for us. Because He loves us, He sent His only Son to die in our place to pay the debt for our sins. He did this so that we could have a relationship with Him and be saved from His wrath and damnation. He gave us life and freedom. He has given us everything that we have. Take time in the midst of sorrow to praise Him for who He is and what He has done for you.

For as a young man marries a virgin, so your sons will marry you; and as the bridegroom rejoices over the bride, so your God will rejoice over you.
Isaiah 62:5

~

Think of the joy of a wedding. The bride and groom have spent so much time planning and dreaming of this day. It is the pinnacle of their love and love story. They have longed for each other and now they are finally one. Imagine their joy! You can see the anticipation in the groom's face as he watches his bride come down the aisle. How he rejoices over her on their wedding night when they are truly united. That is how God rejoices over you. It is no exaggeration. You are His bride and He greatly delights in you. And He doesn't lose His fervor when the honeymoon wears off. He maintains that passion for you. It is not too good to be true. It is truth. Bask in His love and passion. Allow Him to delight in you.

> *The Lord is my light and my salvation, whom shall I fear? The Lord is the refuge of my life, whom shall I dread?*
> *Psalm 27:1*

~

If God is your light, then He is your guide. He helps you see, or rather you see life through Him. He is your shield/visor, your candle, your map/guide book, your glasses. If He is all these things, why are you afraid? If He is your salvation, then you have been saved from sin, hell, and judgment. He is the reason that you are righteous and justified. He will sanctify you and make you holy. If He has already saved you, why are you afraid? If He is the defense and refuge of your life, then you can and should run to Him for help, protection and wisdom. It is He that protects you, guides you, sustains you, fulfills and rejuvenates you, takes care of you, and provides for you. If He is your sanctuary, why are you afraid? Run to Him. Make Him your light and refuge, let Him be your salvation. Stop trying to do it yourself when He has already done it for you.

Every good thing given and every perfect gift is from above, coming down from the Father of lights, with whom there is no variation or shifting shadow. In exercise of His good will He brought us forth by the word of truth, so that we would be a kind of first fruits among His creatures.
James 1:17-18

~

God is unchanging and completely good. There is no evil in Him. He is the father of all good things and of light. Every good thing we have, every blessing, every breath of life is a gift from Him. He created us because He is loving. Think about that. He created you specifically because He loves you and delights in you. As one of His chosen, a Christian, He created you to have a taste of His future glory that you will be a part of in the life to come. Take time to step back and think about every blessing you have now or have ever received. They are gifts from the One Who made you. He planned to give them to you long before you were born. He also planned what you would look like and who you would be, unlike any other. You are special to Him because He made you that way.

Bless the Lord, O my soul, and all that is within me, bless His holy name. Bless the Lord, O my soul, and forget none of His benefits; Who pardons all your iniquities, Who heals all your diseases; Who redeems your life from the pit, Who crowns you with lovingkindness and compassion; Who satisfies your years with good things, so that your youth is renewed like the eagle.
The Lord performs righteous deeds and judgments for all who are oppressed. He made known His ways to Moses, His acts to the sons of Israel.
The Lord is compassionate and gracious; slow to anger and abounding in lovingkindness. He will not always strive with us, nor will He keep His anger forever. He has not dealt with us according to our sins, nor rewarded us according to our iniquities. For as high as the heavens are above the earth, so great is His lovingkindness toward those who fear Him. As far as the east is from the west, so far has He removed our transgressions from us. Just as a father has compassion on his children, so the Lord has compassion on those who fear Him. For He Himself knows our frame; He is mindful that we are but dust. As for man, his days are like grass; as a flower of the field, so he flourishes. When the wind has passed over it, it is no more, and its place acknowledges it no longer. But the lovingkindness of the Lord is from everlasting to everlasting on those who fear Him, and

His righteousness to children's children, to those who keep His covenant and remember His precepts to do them. The Lord has established His throne in the heavens, and His sovereignty rules over all. Bless the Lord, you His angels, mighty in strength, who perform His word, obeying the voice of His word! Bless the Lord, all you His hosts, you who serve Him, doing His will. Bless the Lord, all you works of His, in all places of His dominion; bless the Lord, O my soul!
Psalm 103

~

This psalm is a great refresher for the soul. Remember what God has done for you. He has forgiven your sins. He has healed your body. He has redeemed you from hell and condemnation. He has showered you with love, grace, and compassion. He blesses your life with good things and refreshes your soul and spirit. Remember His ways. He is just and righteous, kind and compassionate; gracious and loving. He is not angry, resentful or bitter. He has shown you mercy and grace. His love is unending and He has permanently forgiven you. He won't take it back. He is the best Father we could ever have. Remember who you are. You are frail and small. Our glory does not last. We grow old quickly and leave no (physical) trace of our existence. Yet God loves us unconditionally and eternally. Remember who He is. He is the King over all creation and created beings. He has power and control over everything. He rules on high. Everything is called to praise Him: the heavenly angels who are still under His will, the whole contingent of the heavenly host that serves Him, every created being on this earth and the whole universe which He has brought into existence. Praise Him!

Are not two sparrows sold for a cent? And yet not one of them will fall to the ground apart from your Father. But the very hairs on your head are all numbered. So do not fear, for you are more valuable than many sparrows.
Matthew 10:29-31

~

Watch the sparrows. Not much bigger than a mouse, they hop around looking for seeds or small nuts to eat and are carefree and unafraid. They don't seem to notice that they are less colorful or attractive and incredibly smaller than most other birds or animals. They just keep on with their business, doing what they can. They are quite insignificant, and yet God knows when each one dies. With all His responsibilities, He still pays attention to a little sparrow. Are you not at least equal to if not greater than a sparrow? You may think that you are insignificant, unimportant or even worthless. But God still pays attention to you, even if it doesn't always seem like it. He is aware of your every move, word, and thought. You are valuable and precious to Him because He made you, and planned you as you are because He delights in you. So ask yourself, how valuable is He to you? How much time and attention do you give Him? If you are not listening to Him, how can He encourage and comfort you? He may be giving you blessings that you are not even aware of because you are focusing on your troubles and not on Him. Take some time to evaluate your life. What has God done for you? What blessings do you have? Cultivate a mind-set of gratitude toward your Maker.

> *Why are you in despair, O my soul? And why have you become disturbed within me?*
> *Hope in God, for I shall yet praise Him, the help of my countenance and my God.*
> Psalm 42:11

~

Many people have been depressed, even in despair. Life is hard and can be very difficult to deal with. But we don't have to let that overwhelm us. Why? How? Our hope is in God. He is our helper; He is the One that we should run to for safety and guidance. He is our salvation; because of His love and mercy we are no longer under condemnation. We don't have to be afraid because He has conquered everything. Death is no longer frightening. If our hope is in God then we have no reason to be continually cast down or hopeless. Yes, life will get us down once in a while, but we shouldn't stay there very long. As Marilla said in Anne of Green Gables, "To despair is to turn your back on God."[ii] Despair and depression are ultimately the result of giving up on God. It is not having faith that He is in control and will save you. Don't let that be your legacy. Hope in God. Focus on what He has already done and promised to do while you wait for Him to work.

For a child will be born to us, a son will be given to us; and the government will rest on His shoulders; and His name will be called Wonderful Counselor, Mighty God, Eternal Father, Prince of Peace.
Isaiah 9:6
~

It makes sense that as the Creator of the whole universe, the One who designed everything with a word, God would also know everything and have the best advice to give in any and every situation. He loves us unconditionally and is much more invested and interested in our lives and situations than even we are. Because of this He cares more than anyone about helping us through whatever we are dealing with. He is the absolute best person to go to for counsel. He knows the best course of action and how best to help us. But He also cares for us so deeply that He WANTS to help us. He desires to have us come to Him. There is no one more trustworthy, knowledgeable or loving to turn to. Have you done that? He is the best choice; He wants you to. What is holding you back? Take that step, reach out in faith and prayer, and go to God with your situation. Turn to Him for help. Unlike any other counselor in the world, He also has the power to do something about it.

If the Lord had not been my help, my soul would soon have dwelt in the abode of silence. If I should say, "My foot has slipped," Your lovingkindness, O Lord, will hold me up. When my anxious thoughts multiply within me, your consolations delight my soul.
Psalm 94:17-19

~

How true is that phrase, "my soul would have soon dwelt in the abode of silence." You are not the only one to have felt so tormented, so lost, so despairing, that you almost could not voice or even comprehend the depth of your sorrow. There are others who have felt this way as well. Christ Himself felt this. You are not alone. Without God we have no hope—literally and figuratively. There truly is no hope apart from God. We feel hopeless and helpless when we are apart from Him. Not that He ever leaves us, but we can forsake fellowship with Him. But even in that, God is faithful. He will help us up. He will not let us fall. Trust in Him. Rest in His loving kindness and find strength there. Many times have I been bombarded with anxious, worrying, disturbing thoughts. It seemed as if everything would fall apart, that it was hopeless. It can be overwhelming. But if we spend time with God, He will renew us and assure us of His love and power. Our time with Him will be our delight. It may not change our circumstances, but it can change our perspective, our mood and our frame of mind so that when we are worried we can trust in Him and rest in His power and presence as we would rest in the arms of a loving parent. Let Him place you on the rock where His security will block the winds of worry. Feel the warmth of His love.

When you pass through the waters, I will be with you, and through the rivers, they will not overflow you. When you walk through the fire, you will not be scorched, nor will the flames burn you. For I am the Lord your God, the Holy One of Israel, your Savior.
Isaiah 43:2-3a

~

God has promised to be with us. No matter what we go through, He will be there beside us. He will not always keep us from suffering, but He has promised to be there to comfort and guide us as we go through it. He has also promised that we will not be overwhelmed by what we are going through. That is not to say that we will never *feel* overwhelmed. When we do feel this way, it is because we have taken our focus off Him and are looking at what is happening around us. Then we feel inundated because it truly is more than we can handle. But it is not more than God can handle. So if we keep our focus on He who has overcome the world we will not be over taken. We may go through some very difficult times, but He has promised to take us through them. He is your God, your Savior. He will do what He has promised. Remember to take refuge in Him. Let Him carry you.

The Lord your God is in your midst, a victorious warrior. He will exult over you with joy. He will be quiet in His love, He will rejoice over you with shouts of joy.
Zephaniah 3:17

~

God is with you. He has not, and will not, forsake you. He will always be near you. He has conquered death and Satan and has the power to protect you. You are a delight to Him, so much so that He is joyful because of you. You make Him so glad that He sings songs of joy. He rests in that quiet ecstasy of complete satisfaction over you. In you is His delight. You make Him so happy that He can't help Himself but shouts His love for you to the entire world. Believe it and bask in His love.

He will swallow up death for all time and the Lord God will wipe tears away from all faces and He will remove the reproach of His people from all the earth for the Lord has spoken.
Isaiah 25:8

~

Death has no power over God. He is mightier and more powerful than any thing, being or action. Nothing can defeat or overpower God. When we trust and believe in Him we inherit that trait and cannot be defeated by death. It doesn't mean that we won't die. All creatures on earth must die because they are mortal. But death is not the end. It is a doorway we go through passing from this life to the next as from one room to another. Once we pass that doorway, though, it is demolished and we cannot go back through it (death) again because we have come into God's kingdom where there is nothing bad or evil. There will be no sadness, no pain, no death, no loss and no separation. All who enter there will be forever inseparable from God. We will eventually be given new bodies that will not be corrupted or tainted. They will not grow old, deteriorate or become diseased. We will have reached perfection in Christ there. We will have no more sorrow or humiliation, no more disappointment or rejection, only love and joy and peace.

"No more crying there, we are going to see the king!
No more dying there, we are going to see the king!
Hallelujah! Hallelujah! We're going to see the king!"[iii]

But God who comforts the depressed, comforted us by the coming of Titus.
2 Corinthians 7:6
~

God comforts the depressed, or those who are down in spirit or humiliated. He lifts up those who are cast down. He gives us grace and joy. He lifts up our heads, so that we are not brought down and consumed by what is around us, so that we can be engulfed in His love and resilient to the evil around us. He may not take away the evil, but He helps us to bear it if we allow Him. He may not send us "Titus", but He has given us a Comforter, the Holy Spirit, who is our mouthpiece or connection to God. God also gives us other forms of comfort through other people to lift our spirits and come alongside us to lighten the load. It may be a child whose innocence gives us some joy, a friend who calls just to see how we are doing, or a stranger whose kind word or act helps ease the pain for a little while. God will not leave us to wallow in the dark alone and helpless. All we have to do is call on Him and He will lift us up.

> *For just as the sufferings of Christ are ours in abundance, so also our comfort is abundant through Christ. But if we are afflicted, it is for your comfort and salvation, or if we are comforted it is for your comfort, which is effective in the patient enduring of the same sufferings which we also suffer.*
> *2 Corinthians 1:5-6*

~

What we suffer for Christ will be proportionate to the comfort we receive from Him. Remember He is not a harsh or cruel master that is slack in love or comfort. He does not allow us to go through more than we are capable of handling with His help. Whatever we are going through, we do not suffer alone because God is always there to comfort us. Fellow believers are there to help us in our trials as well. That is some of the good which comes from our trials. Now we are able to relate to others who have gone, or will go, through the same thing. We can and should comfort others in their time of suffering. And in turn we may need comfort in the future. This partnership of believers helps us to build unity and encourage each other in patient endurance. So don't despair, feel sorry for yourself, or think that no one knows what you are going through. You are not alone in this. Look to God for comfort and allow fellow believers to join with you, to share your burden and help you through this time.

"Do not fear...men of Israel, I will help you,"
declares the Lord, "and your Redeemer is the Holy
One of Israel."
Isaiah 41:14

~

God is our Redeemer, He will help us. He would do it even if He were a selfish god because if one has redeemed something, one does what is necessary to protect and sustain/help what has been redeemed. It would be in His best interest to do so, just as a stockbroker takes care of the investments he has carefully made. But God is more than this. First, He is a loving, good and gracious God. He is incapable of selfishness. It is His character and nature to *do* good and to *be* loving. So He will do even more than what is required because of His nature. Second, He redeemed us not because it would profit Him, but because He loves us. He did it for *our* good, not for His. And someone who does something out of love will do infinitely more than one who has done something merely for profit. So fear not. Your loving, infinitely-good Father has redeemed you and promises to help you because He is good and He loves you. Find peace in His love and goodness.

"Shout for joy, O barren one, you who have borne no child; break forth into joyful shouting and cry aloud, you who have not travailed; for the sons of the desolate one will be more numerous than the sons of the married woman," says the Lord. "Enlarge the place of your tent; stretch out the curtains of your dwellings, spare not; lengthen your cords and strengthen your pegs. For you will spread abroad to the right and to the left. And your descendants will possess nations and will resettle the desolate cities. Fear not, for you will not be put to shame; and do not feel humiliated, for you will not be disgraced; but you will forget the shame of your youth, and the reproach of your widowhood you will remember no more. For your husband is your Maker, Whose name is the Lord of hosts; and your Redeemer is the Holy One of Israel, Who is called the God of all the earth. For the Lord has called you, like a wife forsaken and grieved in spirit, even like a wife of one's youth when she is rejected," says your God. "For a brief moment I forsook you, but with great compassion I will gather you. In an outburst of anger I hid My face from you for a moment, but with everlasting lovingkindness I will have compassion on you," says the Lord your Redeemer. "For this is like the days of Noah to Me, when I swore that the waters of Noah would not flood the earth again; so

*I have sworn that I will not be angry with you nor will I rebuke you. For the mountains may be removed and the hills may shake, but My lovingkindness will not be removed from you, and My covenant of peace will not be shaken,"
says the Lord who has compassion on you.
"O afflicted one, storm-tossed, and not comforted, behold, I will set your stones in antimony, and your foundations I will lay in sapphires. Moreover, I will make your battlements of rubies, and your gates of crystal, and your entire wall of precious stones. All your sons will be taught of the Lord; and the well-being of your sons will be great. In righteousness you will be established; you will be far from oppression, for you will not fear; and from terror, for it will not come near you. If anyone fiercely assails you it will not be from Me. Whoever assails you will fall because of you. Behold, I Myself have created the smith who blows the fire of coals and brings out a weapon for its work; and I have created the destroyer to ruin. No weapon that is formed against you will prosper; and every tongue that accuses you in judgment you will condemn. This is the heritage of the servants of the Lord, and their vindication is from Me,"
declares the Lord.
Isaiah 54*

~

Do not fear because of your trials, do not sorrow because of your suffering. God will bless you richly. He will deliver you. He is the spouse to the widowed and single. He is the father to the orphan. He is comfort for the needy, strength for the weak, joy for the sorrowful, righteousness for the guilty, refuge for the fearful, inheritance for the lost. He will rescue you from your struggles and enemies. He will remove your disgrace and replace it with beauty and honor. He is your Redeemer and He has promised to have everlasting love, and to shower you with His goodness and kindness forever. Maybe He has been angry, maybe He has allowed pain and suffering, but it will not last forever. His compassion for you is greater than His anger could ever be. Remember that He created everything, including Satan, and He still has power over him. One day Satan will be permanently bound and punished. Don't lose heart. Instead, bury your heart in the One who can keep it safe, the One with unconditional, everlasting love. Let Him be your comfort, joy, peace, refuge. Let Him heal your heart.

> *Your dead will live, their corpses will rise. You who lie in the dust awake and shout for joy for your dew is as the dew of dawn and the earth will give birth to the departed spirits.*
> *Isaiah 26:19*

~

Death is not the end. Those who die in Christ will awake and arise again. There will be joy again. We have hope in the Lord. The Creator of life is our hope and joy because He is our salvation and victory over death. There will be sorrow in this life, but it will end. There will be joy afterward for those who trust in Christ. Death really is the beginning of true life. Our lives here are dim visions of what is to come because they have been clouded by sin and evil. But after this life there will be no more sin or evil or death. There will only be life and joy and goodness. Take heart, for He has overcome the world.

Do not fear for I am with you. Do not anxiously look about for I am your God. I will strengthen you, surely I will help you, surely I will uphold you with my righteous right hand.
Isaiah 41:10

~

If God, the Creator of the universe and Master of all creation, is with you, what have you to be afraid of? If He is your God, why would you worry about what may happen, or is happening, to you? He is in control of everything. Nothing happens without His knowledge; He cannot be taken by surprise. So nothing can happen to you that He doesn't know about, and He has promised not to let you be overwhelmed. What have you to fear? He promises to strengthen you so that you can endure and withstand. He promises to help you so that you can make it through. He promises to uphold you so that you will not fall. Trust in Him. He will not fail.

> *How great is Your goodness which you have stored up for those who fear You, which You have wrought for those who take refuge in You, before the sons of men!*
> *Psalm 31:19*

~

God stores up goodness for us. Think about that. He has a special storage unit just for the blessings He has planned to give you. How special are you to Him that He puts that much thought and effort into you! It is full of things He has made, just for you, because He loves you! And this does not mean that He stores them up to keep them from you, rather think of Him finding all the good things He can for you and having a special place to keep them so they will be ready for you at the perfect time. God is wholly good, and has promised to work things out for our good. Trust in His goodness. If He were not good, He would not be God. Is there a catch? No, all that He requires from us is to trust Him, to fear Him, to take refuge in Him. So trust Him, fear Him, take refuge in Him and see what He has stored up for you!

The name of the Lord is a strong tower, the righteous runs into it and is safe.
Proverbs 18:10

~

In Biblical times, towers were fortresses, places of refuge from enemies. The name of the Lord is a strong tower. He is faithful, powerful, merciful, and wise. There is complete strength in Him. Those who run to Him, take refuge in Him, are safe because He is good. He is powerful enough to defeat our enemies and wise enough to guide us. He has mercy enough to forgive our sins, and continue to love us regardless of what we have done. He is faithful enough to trust implicitly. Run to Him and be safe.

God's Sovereignty over Suffering

"It is the ability of God to so arrange diverse human actions to fulfill His purpose that makes His sovereignty marvelous yet mysterious."

Jerry Bridges[iv]

> *Blessed be the God and Father of our Lord Jesus Christ, who according to His great mercy has caused us to be born again to a living hope through the resurrection of Jesus Christ from the dead, to obtain an inheritance which is imperishable and undefiled and will not fade away, reserved in heaven for you, who are protected by the power of God through faith for a salvation ready to be revealed in the last time. In this you greatly rejoice, even though now for a little while, if necessary, you have been distressed by various trials, so that the proof of your faith, being more precious than gold which is perishable, even though tested by fire, may be found to result in praise and glory and honor at the revelation of Jesus Christ; and though you have not seen Him, you love Him, and though you do not see Him now, but believe in Him, you greatly rejoice with joy inexpressible and full of glory, obtaining as the outcome of your faith the salvation of your souls.*
> *1 Peter 1:3-9*

~

God has saved those who believe in Him from destruction. He sent Christ to be the perfect sacrifice for all sin so that those who believe in Him could have an eternal relationship with Him, rather than being separated from Him because of our sin. After Christ died, God raised Him from the dead. Because He is alive today we have hope of eternal life. Death will not be the end, but the doorway to paradise. This is our hope! This passage brings comfort because it 1-shows God's love, 2-shows that we are God's children (who will receive an inheritance from Him), 3-proves that these troubles will end and we will eventually live in paradise with God, and 4-shows that we are protected by God because of our faith. This is the truth that our hope and joy are based on. We also learn that our troubles are "necessary" because they test our faith to prove that it is real. It is proof for us that our faith is genuine so that we don't need to be nagged by doubt. That in turn will glorify God. Because of all this, we should have a joy so great that we are speechless and can't help but glorify God. As a result of our faith, we will eventually have our salvation completed when we reach heaven. How great a joy!

> *You who have shown me many troubles and distresses will revive me again and will bring me up again from the depths of the earth.*
> Psalm 71:20

~

God never promises that we will be safe from bad things, or that we won't have trouble and suffering. Actually, it is the opposite. He said we will go through trouble and suffering. God allows us to suffer the consequences of our actions. He also allows the repercussions of others' actions to affect us. This is not because He is mean or doesn't care. It is because we are sinful and have the freedom to choose what we do. He also allows the natural flow of life to happen whether it is the consequence of someone's actions, accident or illness. Does He want us to be hurt and to suffer? No. But He doesn't want us to sin either, and He gives us the freedom to choose what we do. We may never know the reason why we suffer some tragedy that seems to be no cause of our own. We have to trust that God has our best interest in mind and will not allow us to go through more than we (with Him) can handle. He is our hope, our rock to cling to. When the storm passes He will pull us from the water and set our feet back on dry land. He will give us the strength to keep going and refresh us when we are weary. Cling to His truth and salvation, and wait for the storm to pass.

And we know that God causes all things to work together for good to those who love God, to those who are called according to His purpose.
Romans 8:28

~

First, God is in control of everything. He is more powerful than anything or anyone. He knows everything. Nothing happens without His knowledge and consent. He can cause or prevent whatever circumstances He wants to, but He does not always interfere with the natural course of life. He allows sin to have its consequences. Second, this verse has a clause that says "for those who love God." Not all people love God. Many have rejected Him and His sacrifice to save them. In essence, they have demanded that God not help them. God wants to help everyone, and He gladly helps those who have accepted Him, but He can't and won't help those who have rejected Him. Third, many people think this verse means that if they love God, He will make their lives smooth and they will be happy. That is not what this verse means. The "good" that this verse talks about is not happiness. It is talking about our holiness and sanctification, the process by which God makes us perfect (that is only completed when we reach heaven.) Many are disappointed because even though they love God they suffer, bad things happen and their lives are not perfect. God tells us that we will suffer. We need to look for what God may be teaching us in our suffering. Look for the lesson to be learned or the flaw that God is perfecting through this trial. Try keeping a journal of your sufferings for the purpose of finding the lesson so that you can strive for that, seeking to gain that refining work in us.[v] I think we would suffer much less if we openly sought to be taught by God. If we actively worked to get rid of what is not holy and pure in our lives, God may not have to put us through as much suffering in order to learn those lessons. Submit yourself to God's teaching. In the midst of your sorrow, look for what can be learned and perfected in yourself. Even Jesus learned obedience through suffering.

The Lord will accomplish what concerns me. Your lovingkindness, O Lord, is everlasting. Do not forsake the works of Your hands.
Psalm 138:8

~

God will not stop doing what He has started. When He starts a project He finishes it. He doesn't get bored or tired with the people within whom He is working. He doesn't give up on His plans. He completes them. He made you for a specific purpose with a specific plan in mind. His whole plan is to take you as you are and make you like Him. His purpose is to gradually perfect you. He won't get bored with you, decide you're not worth the effort, or give up on you. You are precious to Him and His love is everlasting. His compassion will not fail. He will not forsake you. You are worth it to Him.

For those who He foreknew He also predestined to become conformed to the image of His Son so that He would be the first born among many brethren; and these whom He predestined, He also called; and these whom He called, He also justified; and these whom He justified, He also glorified.
Romans 8:29-30

~

He planned for you to know Him and be saved. And because He planned it, it happened. There are no ifs or maybes. God speaks and it happens. He planned to save you and make you in His image, to perfect you until you are perfect. He won't stop halfway or do a mediocre job. He will <u>perfect</u> you until you are perfect as He is. Because you believe in Him and what He did, you have been justified. You now have Christ as your representative and your past is literally behind Him. He cannot see it anymore. When He looks at you He sees Christ and His sacrifice and righteousness. And because you have been justified in salvation, you will be glorified. When you get to heaven you will be given a new body, without scar or blemish, eternally youthful and painless. Your soul will also be perfected and you will neither cry nor remember pain any longer. He has done this because He loves you, and you love Him as a result.

> *I sought the LORD, and He answered me, and
> delivered me from all my fears.*
> Psalm 34:4

~

God is in control of everything. He has the power to deal with anything that comes along. He loves you and wants to help you. But He won't barge in and work unless you ask Him to, unless you invite Him into your life and surrender all control to Him. He won't force you. He patiently waits for you to turn to Him. That is the key to this verse. David sought God's help; THEN God answered him and rescued him, not before. Until we do that, <u>we</u> are on the throne of our lives. Essentially we have God bound so that He can't do anything. He remains that way until we surrender control of our lives. It's not that we have any power to keep Him from doing something because we don't. He wants us to want Him. Do you want Him? Have you made Him the King of your life? Maybe you've let things slip and you've started taking back the reins. Take some time to surrender your life back to God. Seek His help, but also seek His lordship over your life. And let Him deal with it.

> *Declaring the end from the beginning, and from ancient times things which have not been done, saying, "My purpose will be established and I will accomplish all My good pleasure"... Truly I have spoken, truly I will bring it to pass. I have planned it, I will do it.*
> *Isaiah 46:10-11*

~

God says in the previous verse, "I am God and there is no one like Me." No other god, person or idol can compare with Him. He is eternal, all-powerful, and almighty. He is the only One who has existed for all eternity and knows all things. He said that He will accomplish His purpose. He cannot go back on His word; it would be contrary to His nature and He would not be God if He did. So He <u>will</u> continue to perfect you and bring good into your life as He said He would. As He has spoken, so He will do. His words are so powerful that a whole universe comes into existence at a word. The Bible is His Word, so think of how much power the Bible has. That is why memorizing scripture is so important and quoting it when Satan tempts or attacks you will send him fleeing. The Bible is part of our power source from God. It is through the Bible that God heals us, and the Bible has so much authority because it is the Word of God. It has so much more power than the words of any person or counselor standing by themselves no matter how important or well studied they are. It is through God and His Word that healing comes. As God said in the Bible so it will be. Claim the promises of the Bible. Take comfort in their assurance.

And He said, "If you will give earnest heed to the voice of the LORD your God, and do what is right in His sight, and give ear to His commandments, and keep all His statutes, I will put none of the diseases on you which I have put on the Egyptians; for I, the LORD, am your healer."
Exodus 15:26

~

There is an important clause here. God's healing is somewhat conditional. He is assuredly the great Healer and Physician, but He doesn't heal everyone and everything. At this point in Exodus, the Israelites were just setting out from Egypt, and already beginning to lose their zeal for God. He knew how they would be in the future so He laid down some rules for them and what the consequences of their actions would bring. As Christians, we are not dependant on the Mosaic Law for salvation. But we are still supposed to obey God. He knows that living in disobedience will bring pain and suffering. His laws were designed to protect us from that. It's a simple cause and effect equation. Our obedience also shows our allegiance to God. If we are rebellious, it shows that we have only "believed" in God to be saved from hell. If we truly believe, serve and obey God, then we will naturally be spared from the consequences of sin. Many Christians feel like God doesn't hear their prayers, or has abandoned them, and the reason is because they are not whole-heartedly serving Him. There is unrepented sin in their lives creating a barrier between them and God. He wants to help and heal us, but we often hinder or prevent His help because of our sin. It's not that we earn or deserve healing by being obedient. But a direct result of our sin is the prevention of healing, just like kicking a rock hurts our feet. In this verse, God is explaining how this process works. If we are true to God, the flow of healing will be open. But if we are rebellious, we are blocking the door to that healing. This does not mean that if you aren't healed physically, then you have done something wrong. Sometimes God chooses not to give physical healing for His greater purposes. But we still need openness in our relationship with God, whatever the outcome. Take some time to examine your life. Ask God to reveal any unrepented sin in your heart, then confess it and restore your relationship with God. Allow Him to heal you.

The Lord will strike Egypt, striking but healing; so they will return to the Lord, and He will respond to them and will heal them.
Isaiah 19:22

~

The troubles and hard times we go through are oftentimes the result of our sin and bad choices, or chastisement from God. Sometimes they are the refining fire melting away the lingering badness in us. But He never allows more than we can handle with Him at our side, and He never does it out of cruelty. To do that would be to go against His character. He does all for our good, even the hard times. We need to trust His promises and keep our hope in Him. We need to turn to Him for comfort and guidance. We need to go to Him for healing. Trials and suffering are not always punishment, but they are always times that we can turn to God and refocus our lives on Him. They are opportunities to see what God can teach us, what transformations He can make in our lives to mold us into His image. Turn to Him, seek His guidance, and see that He is good.

> *Who is there who speaks and it comes to pass,*
> *unless the Lord has commanded it? Is it not from*
> *the mouth of the Most High that both good and ill*
> *go forth?*
> *Lamentations 3:37-38*

~

God is all good and there is no evil in Him. What Jeremiah writes is that God orchestrates both good and bad things. Not that He wants bad things to happen, but He actively allows nature to run its course in storms, and sinful people to do sinful things. He does not always protect the innocent from bad things happening to them. It is harder to accept that a good God would let bad things happen, and we won't always, or even usually, know why. We have to trust that He is all-powerful and all-good and what He has in mind is best for those who trust Him. He is in control and knows everything that is going to happen, and will not let you go through more than you can bear. It is through trusting Him that we find peace and comfort. We can do nothing without Him allowing it and knowing about it before hand. Go to God and let Him to take care of your life.

I will rejoice over them to do them good and will faithfully plant them in this land with all My heart and all My soul.
Jeremiah 32:41

~

God had passed judgment on Israel, and allowed them to be taken captive and enslaved and suffer horrendous atrocities at the hands of cruel and merciless men. He did this to His beloved, chosen people. Why? They had rejected Him and His laws. But for all He allowed them to go through, it wasn't a sign of indifference or cruelty. He allowed them to be punished when they refused to heed His warnings, but He still loved them and wept over their destruction. Maybe you feel like you have been abandoned, forsaken by God, allowed to go through the worst desolation, humiliation, or pain. This doesn't mean that God no longer cares about you. That is a lie devised by Satan, the father of lies, to keep you miserable and make you despair. We may never know why we go through the hard times that we do, but God will make it work out for our benefit in the long run. He can see our future and knows what is best for us. We have to trust that truth. And God will say of you as He did of Israel: He will rejoice over you, do you good, and put you in the best place. He will reward your suffering someday, even if that day does not come until heaven. The pain will not last forever.

> *He will not allow your foot to slip. He who keeps you will not slumber. Behold He who keeps Israel will neither slumber nor sleep.*
> *Psalm 121:3-4*

~

God knows what is going to happen to you. He has planned the whole course of your life. Your circumstances or actions will never surprise Him. He will guard your path and your steps. Bad things may happen but nothing is out of God's control or His power to take care of. There will never be a time that you are out of His sight, when you can do something that He does not know about. He doesn't sleep. He is always watching over you. He won't turn His back on you or close His eyes so that He can't see you. You are always in His vision. Even when it feels like you are completely alone, God is always there, always watching. You are never alone.

In the day of prosperity be happy, but in the day of adversity consider – God has made the one as well as the other so that man will not discover anything that will be after him.
Ecclesiastes 7:14

~

In prosperity we have reason to be happy, obviously. God has blessed us and life is good. But in adversity…? It did not happen that God made prosperity and someone else is in control of adversity. He cannot do anything evil or sinful, but He ordains everything that happens. He is all-powerful, all-knowing, and all-in-control. Does He want us to sin or suffer? No, but He won't stop us from sinning, from suffering the consequences of our sin, or always protect us from the consequences of others' sin. He knew everything as it would happen before He formed the earth. By His design, we won't know the result or outcome of anything, or what will happen next. But because we cannot see the whole picture, we also cannot censure what God is doing or has done. No one can advise or correct God. It is through adversity that He develops fruit in us. It is only through adversity that we can grow in holiness, perseverance, and dependence on God. Trust God, for He holds your future. He knows what will happen and will work it out for your benefit.

For the Lord of hosts has planned, and who can frustrate it? And as for His stretched-out hand, who can turn it back?
Isaiah 14:27

~

No one changes God's plans. His plans cannot be frustrated. Satan cannot send some demons in guerilla warfare to stop you from getting some blessing or source of strength from God, nor can he mess up the plans God has for you or make bad things happen against God's will. If God has ordained it, it will happen. Period. God knows more than any, is more powerful than any, and none can out-smart or surprise Him. Take refuge and trust the God that none can thwart.

Even from eternity I am He, and there is none who can deliver out of my hand, I act and who can reverse it?
Isaiah 43:13

~

God has always existed. There was never a time before Him and there will never be a time beyond Him. He is eternal and time does not affect Him. He is ageless and immune to the passage of time. He existed before there was anything else. He is the Creator of all creation. He is the only being that was not created. He just is. He exists and accomplishes His will. He planned you from the beginning and has a purpose for you. His actions cannot be changed nor do they ever end so that He is frustrated. He could squash Satan and his whole demonic force with one finger. Satan cannot triumph over God because Satan was created by God. He cannot do anything to you that God doesn't allow. You are under God's protection, the protection of the Almighty and ever-existent. Take comfort in that assurance.

Job
~

Almost every writing about suffering includes Job's. He went through so much, in one day: all 10 of his children were killed, he lost all of his livestock and the majority of his servants. He eventually suffered painful physical disease as well. To top it off, his wife told him to just curse God and die, and his friends chided him for insisting that he was not hiding some sin for which God was punishing him. The important thing to note about Job's story is that he truly did not deserve any of what happened to him. The whole purpose of his suffering was for God to prove Job's integrity and uprightness to Satan. In cynical terms, Satan bet God that Job would turn against Him if he suffered enough. God disagreed and "took the wager" as it were, allowing Satan to torture him, but only so far. God was still in control. And yet, Job never knew why he suffered. And he did not suffer because of anything he or anyone else did. There is not always a rhyme or reason to what happens, but God is always in control. An interesting thing to note is that immediately after the initial grief of his loss, he turned and praised God. He knew and understood that everything he had was a gift from God and that God gives and takes away at His own discretion. He was able to withstand the pain by keeping a realistic, open-handed view of life and his relationship with God. Let that be your model for suffering!

Oh the depth of the riches both of the wisdom and knowledge of God! How unsearchable are His judgments and unfathomable His ways!
Romans 11:33

~

God is eternal, does not have a beginning or end, knows everything and is everywhere. How could we possibly understand Him? Resist the temptation to ask why something has happened. God does not always tell us the reason. We cannot fathom the intricacies of how everything in life fits together. If He did tell us we wouldn't understand. Sometimes He is teaching us to trust Him. If we knew the reasons for everything we wouldn't have to trust God to provide and protect. If we knew it ahead of time, we might interfere with God's plan by trying to make it happen, or by doing it our own way. So trust the all-powerful, infinite God to take care of you and rest in the knowledge that He knows what is going on.

> *As for God, His way is blameless, the word of the Lord is tried, He is a shield to all who take refuge in Him.*
> *Psalm 18:30*

~

God's way is perfect. He can do no wrong because of His character. He also knows everything that will happen, and has planned everything to work out for our best. We could not possibly find a way of doing something better than God, and it is arrogant to try. His word has been tested. He cannot break a promise or go back on His word. He is completely trustworthy. Because of these things we can trust Him implicitly. He will never let us down. And if we do trust in Him, He will be a shield and protector for us, but we have to take refuge in Him. Take some time to look at your life. Are you trusting God completely, in every area? If there are some areas where you don't trust God entirely, or at all, ask Him to help you trust Him. Be committed to making an effort to trust Him. He will reward your faithfulness.

*Heal me, O Lord, and I will be healed; save me and
I will be saved, for You are my praise.*
Jeremiah 17:14

~

God is the sole source of true healing. He is the only One that can fully understand your pain; the only One with enough power and wisdom to solve your problem and heal your wound. He made you and knows what to do. The key is trusting Him to do it. Give Him control over your life and situation. He is the only One that can save you because He is the only One through Whom salvation comes. It's not that help cannot be found through others. Sometimes counseling is needed, but it has to be based on God's healing power and not man's wisdom. Notice the promise in this verse, "heal me and I <u>will</u> be healed." It will happen. Make Him your praise and delight. Make Him your great Physician and Healer. He can do miracles beyond your imagination so don't limit Him merely to human methods. Ask Him to do the impossible and trust Him for healing.

The king's heart is like channels of water in the hand of the Lord, He turns it wherever He wishes.
Proverbs 21:1

~

God is completely in control of His universe. Granted, He has given us free will and allows us to make our own choices, but His world is never out of His control. Think of how many times you narrowly escaped something bad or some random accident! God was protecting you. He was moving your car, or stopping a rock, or whatever almost happened. He was actively intervening. God works everything according to His will and purpose, and for your benefit, because your good is His will. Our nation, local governments, and even society, may seem as if they are heading in the wrong direction, but God is still in control. He knows what will happen in the future. So no matter how bad things look, God has a plan and He has control.

For truly in this city there were gathered together against Your holy servant Jesus, whom You anointed, both Herod and Pontius Pilate, along with the Gentiles and the peoples of Israel, to do whatever Your hand and Your purpose predestined to occur.
Acts 4:27-28

~

Many people plotted to kill Jesus at several points in His life, beginning with Herod in His childhood, and the Pharisees throughout His ministry. But no matter what plot they devised, Christ was not killed until the time the Father had ordained, in the manner He foretold. Notice it says they were gathered together against Him, but they could only do whatever God's hand and purpose predestined to occur. They were all acting according to God's plan whether they knew it or not. There are many places in the Gospels where it says that the crowd or the Pharisees moved to seize Jesus but couldn't because He was hidden, for His time had not yet come. God made everything work according to His plan then, and He will do no less in your own life. He had everything orchestrated from the beginning and no one can ruin His plans. Trust in Him and His sovereign will. Have peace in the knowledge that He loves you and holds you in the palm of His hand.

Thus says the Lord, "In a favorable time I have answered You, and in a day of salvation I have helped You; and I will keep You and give You for a covenant of the people, to restore the land, to make them inherit the desolate heritages; saying to those who are bound, 'Go forth,' to those who are in darkness, 'Show yourselves.' Along the roads they will feed, and their pasture will be on all bare heights. They will not hunger or thirst, nor will the scorching heat or sun strike them down; for He who has compassion on them will lead them and will guide them to springs of water. I will make all My mountains a road, and My highways will be raised up. Behold, these will come from afar; and lo, these will come from the north and from the west, and these from the land of Sinim." Shout for joy, O heavens! And rejoice, O earth! Break forth into joyful shouting, O mountains! For the Lord has comforted His people and will have compassion on His afflicted. But Zion said, "The Lord has forsaken me, and the Lord has forgotten me." "Can a woman forget her nursing child and have no compassion on the son of her womb? Even these may forget, but I will not forget you. Behold, I have inscribed you on the palms of My hands; your walls are continually before Me. Your builders hurry; your destroyers and devastators will depart from you. Lift up your eyes and look around; all of them gather together, they come to you. As I live," declares the Lord, "You will surely put on all of them

as jewels and bind them on as a bride. For your waste and desolate places and your destroyed land—surely now you will be too cramped for the inhabitants, and those who swallowed you will be far away. The children of whom you were bereaved will yet say in your ears, 'The place is too cramped for me; make room for me that I may live here.' Then you will say in your heart, 'Who has begotten these for me, since I have been bereaved of my children and am barren, an exile and a wanderer? And who has reared these? Behold, I was left alone; from where did these come?'"
Isaiah 49:8-21

~

In God's time, He will answer. He does not work according to our desired schedule, but to His infinite plan. He knows what is best for you, better than you do yourself. And when His help comes, it is with salvation and restoration. He is a good and gracious Father who gives all we need and more. He is not stingy with His love and gifts. He will have compassion and guide you to restoration. He will bring you "home" to Him and comfort you. Do not think that God has forsaken you. He made you and cherishes you. Only the most cold-hearted parent could completely abandon their child, and God is not like that. Remember, He is kind and loving, and infinitely so. He has "inscribed you on the palm" of His hands. You are tattooed there where He will always see a reminder of you. He has made it impossible to forget you. God sees your trials and will make them as a crown for you. How? By enduring and trusting in Him, you will grow, your character will strengthen, and you will have a deeper relationship with God that will be as obvious as a crown would be. It will adorn you with grace. He will make you victorious. He will bless you beyond your imagination. Hold fast, stay the course, trust in God who will not forsake you!

For the Lord will not reject forever, for if He causes grief, then He will have compassion according to His abundant lovingkindness. For He does not afflict willingly or grieve the sons of men.
Lamentations 3:31-33

~

Sometimes it feels like we have been rejected by God, like He has forgotten or abandoned us, or turned us over to catastrophe. But He is loving and what He does is for our own good. Perhaps it is not really that He has rejected us, but that we have rejected Him, either blatantly or through unrepented sin. Maybe we are suffering the consequences of our own actions, or those of others. God promises that no matter what, it will not last forever. He promises that He will have compassion according to His lovingkindness, which is unending. He does not allow these things because He is cruel, sadistic, or indifferent. He loves you and if you suffer, He allows it because of His just nature, but His love will not allow it to be more than you can bear with His help. Don't lose heart or faith. He is there. He is loving. Run to Him and let Him take care of your troubles and heal your wounds.

But when God, who had set me apart even from my mother's womb and called me through His grace, was pleased (to save me)...
Galatians 1:15

~

Paul is the author of Galatians. If you remember his past, he was the major zealot and persecutor of Christians. He arrested many believers and was a terror to the Christian community in the early days. But God had a plan for him, and he ended up being one of the greatest evangelists of all time. It wasn't because God decided to stop his rampage and so changed him for good, or that God was finally able to get through to him to change his mind. God had a plan all along. Paul had been chosen for that ministry before he was born, which was also long before Christ began His ministry on earth. God knew the details of your life before you even began it. He knows when you will enter a relationship with Him, what your ministry will be and when you will start it, and He knew all of that before you first drew breath. He knows what your future entails. Trust Him with your life, go to Him for counsel, take refuge in the One who holds your future.

By the word of the LORD the heavens were made, and by the breath of His mouth all their host... for He spoke, and it was done; He commanded, and it stood fast.
Psalm 33:6,9

~

God spoke and breathed the universe into existence out of nothing. God is so powerful that even the words He speaks have power to do far more than we could ever imagine. A God that mighty can certainly take care of anything that you may be going through. He is the most powerful being/force ever. He is so powerful that He defeated death in one blow. A being this great doesn't make mistakes. He knows what will come of every action that happens and can plan ahead for anything, and has. He is too wise to make a mistake, and is powerful enough to correct any mistakes you make. You can trust His will and His word. He will take care of you if you will trust in Him. Turn to the most powerful being and let Him take care of your problems. He is mighty enough to do it, and then some.

The lot is cast into the lap, but its every decision is from the LORD.
Proverbs 16:33
~

Casting lots was an Old Testament way of discerning God's will by throwing dice, basically. It was something that the priests would do after a special ceremony. Some thought the outcome was due to the priests instead of God, just as some view rain as a gift from the clouds rather than a gift from God. They would remove the Originator from the equation. But this verse reminds us that regardless of what people think, God is in control. He is not affected by what people think or do. Seek God's will for guidance and trust His wisdom.

Lo, for my own welfare I had great bitterness; it is You who has kept my soul from the pit of nothingness, for You have cast all my sins behind Your back.
Isaiah 38:17

~

God is the One who protects us. Without His grace we are helpless. But if we confess our sins, He will completely wipe them away. He won't just erase them from the book of your life; He will get a brand new page. He <u>chooses</u> not to remember them any more. You are no longer condemned before Him. When He looks at you, He sees His precious Son. You are His child, He will not turn you away. He longs for you to come to Him. Stop your bitterness, come out of hiding, and run to Him. Restore your relationship with your loving Father.

I, even I, am the one who wipes out your transgressions for My own sake, and I will not remember your sins.
Isaiah 43:25

~

This is the epitome of mercy and grace. In no way did the Jews deserve to be forgiven, yet God forgave them. He vowed to not remember their sins. He did it to enlighten us, so that we would know His love and generosity. He did it to show them His trustworthiness, to win their adoration. He wants us to come to Him. He wants to save us. He is not cruel or harsh. And He proves that here. Do not be afraid to come to Him. He does not remember what you have done. It's not because He is forgetful, but because He has <u>chosen</u> not to remember. Confess your sin to Him and be forgiven. Come; restore your relationship with your loving Savior.

> *The unfortunate commits himself to You;*
> *You have been the helper of the orphan.*
> *Psalm 10:14b*

~

God helps those who have no one else. That is why Christianity is growing in third world countries faster than in the developed nations. They <u>need</u> Him. They commit their lives to Him because He is the only one who can help them. He is a father to those who have no father. They know this and turn to Him. This doesn't mean that He changes their circumstances so that they have comfortable lives. He changes their hearts and gives them peace and comfort so that they can bear their hardships. Oh that we privileged could be so fortunate as to truly see our need for Him rather than feeling independent and self sufficient! Pray that God will open your eyes to see your need for Him. Turn to the only One that can help you.

I, even I, am He who comforts you. Who are you that you are afraid of man who dies and of the son of man who is made like grass, that you have forgotten the LORD your Maker, who stretched out the heavens and laid the foundations of the earth, that you fear continually all day long because of the fury of the oppressor, as he makes ready to destroy? But where is the fury of the oppressor?
Isaiah 51:12-13

~

God is our comforter and healer. Look at what He has already done and has promised to do. Why are you worried? Why are you afraid? If God is your God, you have nothing to worry about or be afraid of. So many of our fears are because of another person, but God is more powerful than all people combined. The Bible says that people are like grass. They are alive for a brief time and then they are gone with little left behind. Why would we be afraid of one so insignificant compared to the One who is eternal? Remember the One who made you, who provides for you and takes care of you. Trust in Him, let Him take care of the details of your life and guide you. Give Him your problems and worry.

But the Lord stood with me and strengthened me, so that through me the proclamation might be fully accomplished, and that all the Gentiles might hear; and I was rescued out of the lion's mouth. The Lord will rescue me from every evil deed, and will bring me safely to His heavenly kingdom; to Him be the glory forever and ever. Amen.
2 Timothy 4:17-18

~

Paul had been abandoned and betrayed. Few stood by him. But God did. He never left Paul, rather He strengthened him so that he could finish his mission and take the gospel to all people. God rescued him not only from those who were against him, but also from Satan. Paul knew that God was faithful to defend him. It didn't matter what other people did to or thought about him, God knew the truth about Paul and would save him. Paul eventually died in prison, but he went to heaven, and knew that he would because he believed in Jesus. No one could keep him from spending eternity with God. You may think that is all because he was such a great apostle, but this is all true for every believer. If we have a true, saving belief in who Jesus is, then God will strengthen and save us and we will spend eternity with Him.

Our Response to Suffering

"O Praise God for all you have and trust Him for all you want."

John Wesley[vi]

This is my hope in my affliction that Your word has revived me.
Psalm 119:50

~

The King James translates *revived* as *quickened*. It has a two fold meaning. First is the process of perffection or sanctification, which begins at the time of salvation. There is hope in that because we do not have to stay as helpless sinners, separated from God, under the dominion of sin. We are saved and transformed by God at salvation and that process is begun and developed by God's Word. It is God's Word that speaks to us, helping us to know God and to become holy. The second is consolation. God comforts us through His Word. It is in His word that we read His promises, are reminded of His love and faithfulness, and commiserate with others (including God) who have experienced similar pain. It is through His word that we learn and are reassured that God is ultimately good, has our best interests in mind and has a specific plan for us. Because He has defeated even death, it has no power over us either. Take some time now to read God's word and be renewed and comforted by it.

Your testimonies also are my delight; they are my counselors.
Psalm 119:24

~

The best way we have of knowing God's will, opinion, or thoughts on a subject is in the Bible. We have the word of God written down for us in plain language so that we can read what God has to say. The Bible is the best counseling tool we have available because it plainly and clearly shows us God's will and opinions on any subject, but as with any other piece of counsel, it does no good if it is not used. We have to take God's word and apply it in order to benefit from it. It is good to read your Bible, even better to read it daily, but if it is not applied, it just becomes another book with good ideas, another board on Pinterest full of things you want to try but never do. In order for God's word to truly be a counselor, it also has to be our delight. We have to want it and we have to use it (all of it, not just the verses we like). If you have a favorite exercise activity, you will do it more often, and with more vigor, and so will see more benefit from it than others. That is how it must be with the Bible; otherwise it ends up as that treadmill or workout video that sits in the corner taking up space. You must use it, otherwise it won't help you at all. So get your Bible out, and spend some time with God. Get in there and see what He has to show you.

> *The LORD appeared to him from afar, saying, "I have loved you with an everlasting love; therefore I have drawn you with lovingkindness."*
> Jeremiah 31:3

~

Israel had abandoned God and been exiled and punished for their betrayal, but it wasn't permanent. Just as a father disciplines his children for their disobedience, God disciplines us for ours. It proves that we are His children. And, really, it proves His love because He wants to make us better/perfect rather than leave us in the misery of sin and bad choices. He is love. He always loves us, no matter what. And He draws us back to Him with that love and compassion. Nothing you do or have done is beyond His forgiveness. He has promised to love and forgive. He cannot go back on His word. Trust Him. Go to Him. Repent of what you have done and seek His forgiveness and restoration. Be reconciled to God and enjoy His love again.

> *Therefore if anyone is in Christ, he is a new creature; the old things have passed away; behold, new things have come.*
> *2 Corinthians 5:17*

~

A new creature…it doesn't say rebuilt, patched or fixed. It says <u>new</u>. You are brand new when you become Christ's. You have cast away the old (sin) nature like dirty clothes and have put on Christ, allowing Him to live in you and control your life. He has the power to completely heal you from your sins and wrongs that have been done to you. You don't have to live under them any more. You can be rid of it. They do not have to define or bind you any longer. Let Christ make you new. Seek Him for healing and restoration. He has the power and the desire to make you new, to heal your heart. Let Him do it. Put on Christ and put away the past.

> *Trust in the Lord forever for in God the Lord, we have an everlasting Rock.*
> *Isaiah 26:4*

~

It is so easy when life gets hard to lose sight of God, to focus on the troubles around us, and drown in the sorrow or despair that drags us down engulfing us in our difficulties. Remember Peter when he tried to walk on water? When he focused on the storm and waves around him, he sank into the sea. It was by focusing only on Christ that he was lifted out of the water and had victory over his fear. He was still in the storm, but he was no longer drowning. I've learned that is how depression operated in my life. As long as I focused on myself, what was wrong and what made me sad I became even more depressed. It was like a black hole, sucking up everything around it, consuming even itself, to the point that I was blinded by my depression. I could not remember joy or peace or life without pain. It was not until I took my focus completely off myself, stopped trying to make myself happy and focused entirely on God that I was lifted out of my depression. When you're in sinking sand you cannot pull yourself out of it, you will only sink further by moving. You have to have someone else pull you out. God is the eternal Rock, refuge and fortress that we can cling to for safety and salvation. He is the only One that will last, all others will fade away. He is the only safe One. He is the only One wholly trustworthy. Cast your cares on Him and trust Him for deliverance.

When I am afraid, I will put my trust in You. In God, whose word I praise, in God I have put my trust; I shall not be afraid. What can man do to me?
Psalm 56:3-4

~

There is much in life that can make us afraid. Fear is one of Satan's greatest weapons to keep us defeated. I have been fearful of anything and everything most of my life because I did not truly trust in God. I knew that He loved me and would take care of me. But I didn't fully trust Him. I had some doubts, so I tried to maintain control and that kept me in bondage to fear. In order to overcome fear, and be victorious, I had to fully trust in God. I had to believe that He loved me and had my best interest in mind. You have to believe that He is all-powerful, all-knowing, and all-in-control. Most importantly, you have to believe that Jesus came to earth as a baby, suffered and died as a man, was buried and brought back to life, and is alive today as God, having defeated death and sin. That is the key to peace and victory: His victory.

> *Make sure that your character is free from the love of money, being content with what you have; for He Himself has said, "I WILL NEVER DESERT YOU, NOR WILL I EVER FORSAKE YOU," so that we confidently say, "THE LORD IS MY HELPER, I WILL NOT BE AFRAID. WHAT WILL MAN DO TO ME?"*
> *Hebrews 13:5-6*

If God is always with us, then we are never alone. If God promises to provide everything we need, then we will never go without. If God is our helper, then we don't need to be afraid of anyone. If God is our guide, we will never go astray. God is all of these things and more. It is Who He is and He cannot change. The key is that we have to allow and seek for Him to work in our lives. He won't just barge in uninvited. We have to ask Him for help. The command to be free from love of money means that God provides everything we need (by His standards), so we should be content with what we have because God says it is enough. We should love God more than we love anything else. We should trust God for our needs (I'm not saying we shouldn't work, but that we should trust God that we will have enough). The key is trusting God and being content. Take some time to examine your life and see if you are not trusting God or not content in some area. Turn to God, ask Him to forgive your doubt, and ask Him to help you trust in Him.

"The Lord is my portion," says my soul, "Therefore I have hope in Him." The Lord is good to those who wait for Him, to the person who seeks Him.
Lamentations 3:24-25

~

Our hope comes from God. From Him is our salvation and livelihood. He has given us everything we have. Our hope comes from trusting Him to provide, protect and save. When we do, we can have hope because we have the assurance that He is trustworthy. He is our portion, provision and all that we need. With Him we can have everything good; life, love, joy, peace and more. Without Him we literally have and are nothing. It is when we place our trust in things and people other than God that we lose hope because our trust is not in God alone. How can you really have hope when you are trusting in something that is sure to disappoint you? God won't let you down. He is good to those who wait and seek for Him. We must not be satisfied with anything less than Him. We need to focus solely on Him and make Him the object and subject of our lives.

> *Offer to God a sacrifice of thanksgiving and pay your vows to the Most High; call upon Me in the day of trouble; I shall rescue you, and you will honor Me.*
> *Psalm 50:14-15*

~

There is an order here that is necessary to notice. <u>First</u> he says to offer a sacrifice of thanksgiving and pay your vows to God, <u>then</u> call upon Him. He will rescue you, <u>and</u> you will honor Him. It is important that we always acknowledge God's place and work in our lives. He is the orchestrater of everything. It is because of Him that we exist and have everything that we possess. Even in bad times we need to thank Him for who He is and what He has given us. We need to acknowledge before Him our place, our humble dependant standing, and make ourselves right with Him. Then, when we call on Him, He will rescue us. Not before. He knows our needs for sure, but we have to ask Him. Our relationship with God is no different than with any other person. It needs time and effort to develop and talking to Him is part of that. Why would He do something for someone that didn't care enough about Him to ask for help? That's not to say He wouldn't anyway, but there is a necessary order here. The last step should be a given. When we are rescued or blessed, we are usually very grateful and show our appreciation. That's how it should be with God. We begin and end with thanksgiving. Not only that, but we should also reaffirm our place of dependence on Him. He is the only being that we can safely put on that pedestal or ivory tower because He is the only One that cannot let us down. He is the only One worthy of that honor. Take a moment to thank Him for all the blessings you have and humbly ask God to help you.

> *Lo, for my own welfare I had great bitterness; it is You who has kept my soul from the pit of destruction, for You have cast all my sins behind Your back.*
> *Isaiah 38:17*

~

King Hezekiah of Judah was incredibly ill, and felt that his illness was due to his sin. Yet he turned to God, repented of his sin, and he was healed both physically and spiritually. What you are going through may not be a result of your sin. Indeed, illness usually is not a direct product of sin, nor are tragedies like the loss of a child. But hurts inflicted by yourself or another often are. Mistreatment by a loved one, or pain caused by bad decisions like divorce, are usually the result of someone disobeying God. When God says to do or not do something He has a right to be obeyed. There are consequences for our disobedience. Regardless of whether your pain is a result of sin or not, take some time to ask God to search your life for sin that you haven't repented of. It is vital for maintaining your relationship with God. He has promised that if we turn to Him we will be forgiven. This is a healing like none other and He will always give it.

> *For this reason I also suffer these things, but I am not ashamed; for I know whom I have believed and I am convinced that He is able to guard what I have entrusted to Him until that day.*
> 2 Timothy 1:12

~

Paul, one of the greatest apostles and teachers of the Christian faith, suffered. He had a "thorn in his flesh." Perhaps it was some character defect or physical impediment; maybe a particular temptation that he struggled with. Regardless, he was imperfect, like us, and more than that, God allowed him to continue suffering from that thorn, even though Paul asked to be delivered from it. Paul's affliction was no reflection on his piety, but his reaction to it was. Rather than feeling sorry for himself because of his affliction, or being angry with God for allowing him to suffer, he was not ashamed of it. He did not consider it as something that would hinder him. He worked through it, and even used it to encourage others. How was he able to do that? He trusted God. He was firm in his faith and knew that eternity rested in Christ. What really mattered, his soul/salvation, was firm in Christ and no one could take it from him. His hope was in God, who does not disappoint. And that hope gave him peace, joy, and confidence. Do you trust God with your life and eternal salvation? Do you trust the Creator and Orchestrator of the universe to take care of you? Do you believe that He is able to save you? Take some time to search your heart, and make yourself right with God. Rely on Him for He is the only one trustworthy. Rest in His arms and let Him take care of you.

And we know that God causes all things to work together for good to those who love God, to those who are called according to His purpose.
Romans 8:28

~

This calling to purpose is His calling, essentially to salvation. He planned those who would accept Him and knows who they are before they are even born. God planned that He would save you. Not only that, but He causes all things; good, bad, temptation, sin, disaster, accident, to work out for your good or benefit. Bad things may happen to you, but He will make good come out of it. Even when we mess up, if we repent and turn to Him, He will make good come of it. That doesn't necessarily mean we won't suffer the consequences of sin, but God will make good come from that too. Part of that is being open to correction and direction. We can learn from our mistakes, become wiser and more mature, and learn to follow God as a result. God will perfect and refine us if we allow Him to. An example could be an unwanted pregnancy borne of unmarried sex or rape. The good to come would be the child, precious life born from sin or pain, respectively. Children are a blessing and God never means for them to be a curse or a punishment. Maybe the mother in that circumstance is unable to care for the child; it would be a blessing to its adopted parents, who might be people unable to have children of their own. What a blessing to them!! And that is merely one possible good thing that could come from two specific situations. The opportunities for God to make good happen are endless. That doesn't mean that is why it happened, but it can be a byproduct of the process. Watch for God working in our lives, teaching us to see the good. Look for His work and blessings.

> *I know that You can do all things and that no purpose of yours can be thwarted, "Who is this that hides counsel without knowledge?" Therefore I have declared that which I did not understand, things too wonderful for me which I did not know.*
> *Job 42:2-3*

~

Job, after all his sufferings and sorrow, pushed to the end of frustration by his doubting friends and wife, questioned God and His integrity. God responded by showing Job His awesome glory; all His creation which He had made, the intricacies of life which He orchestrated, and His surpassing knowledge that goes far beyond anything we could ever hope to comprehend. God chastised Job for his insolence, and dared him to try to match up to His almighty worthiness. God's rebuke lasts from chapter 38 through 41 and I encourage you to read those chapters to remind yourself of His awesomeness. By the end of God's rebuke, Job was thoroughly humbled, realizing that he is one insignificant being created by God among all His majesty. And the fact that God would pay any attention to him, let alone hear his prayers, only humbled Job more, leading him to praise God for who He is and to retract and repent of his doubts and accusations. Job never knew why he suffered such awful tragedy, yet still he praised God and trusted Him. It is a valuable lesson to learn. Because of God's awesome greatness, faithfulness, and knowledge, we should accept our circumstances and trust God to take care of us in the midst of them. Take some time to remind yourself how awesome God is, His many blessings to you, and ponder your responses to Him. Have you doubted, questioned, or complained against God? Confess it to Him now. Renew your pledge of trust in Him, and endeavor to accept His will for your life whatever that entails.

> *We have obtained an inheritance, having been predestined according to His purpose who works all things after the counsel of His will to the end that we who were the first to hope in Christ would be to the praise of His glory.*
> Ephesians 1:11-12

~

We have been predestined, or chosen ahead of time, by God. He planned to save each one of us individually. That is His plan. His goal is that we would glorify Him and cause Him to be praised by others. We also have an inheritance through Him because we are His adopted children. That is part of the deal when we are saved; we are added to His family. So, our purpose here on earth is to give God glory, and we do that by doing what the Bible tells us to do (avoiding sin and doing God's work) and also by the way we react to the trials that we face. Complaining and grumbling against God only shows that we are unhappy with our faith, and that we think God isn't doing a good enough job. The world needs to see our trust and reliance in Him. We glorify God by praising Him for His blessings. When we attribute all that we have to God, we are giving Him His due essentially. By showing our faith in Him and not being depressed or down hearted, we show other people that there is something good and different about being a Christian. But our reactions come from the heart. What we say and do is an example of what we believe in our hearts. That is the first area to be addressed. Do you believe that God is good and has your best in mind? Do you trust Him to take care of you? Do you have hope and peace because of His saving grace and love?

Do not fret because of evildoers, be not envious toward wrongdoers. For they will wither quickly like the grass and fade like the green herb. Trust in the Lord and do good; dwell in the land and cultivate faithfulness. Delight yourself in the Lord; and He will give you the desires of your heart. Commit your way to the Lord, trust also in Him, and He will do it. He will bring forth your righteousness as the light and your judgment as the noonday. Rest in the Lord and wait [c]patiently for Him; do not fret because of him who prospers in his way, because of the man who carries out wicked schemes. Cease from anger and forsake wrath; do not fret; it leads only to evildoing. For evildoers will be cut off, but those who wait for the Lord, they will inherit the land. Yet a little while and the wicked man will be no more; and you will look carefully for his place and he will not be there. But the humble will inherit the land and will delight themselves in abundant prosperity. The wicked plots against the righteous and gnashes at him with his teeth. The Lord laughs at him, for He sees his day is coming. The wicked have drawn the sword and bent their bow to cast down the afflicted and the needy, to slay those who are upright in conduct. Their sword will enter their own heart, and their bows will be broken. Better is the little of the righteous than the abundance of many wicked. For the arms of the wicked will be broken, but the Lord sustains the righteous. The Lord knows the days of the blameless, and their inheritance will be forever. They will not be ashamed in the time of evil, and in the days of famine they will have abundance. But the wicked will perish; and the enemies of the Lord will be like the glory of the pastures, they vanish—like smoke they vanish away. The wicked borrows and does not pay back, but the righteous is gracious and gives. For those blessed by Him will inherit the land, but those cursed by Him will be cut off. The steps of a man are established by the Lord, and He delights in his way. When he falls, he will not be hurled headlong, because the Lord is the One who holds his hand. I have been young and now I am old, yet I have not seen the righteous forsaken or his descendants begging bread. All day long he is gracious and lends, and his descendants are a blessing. Depart from evil and do good, so you will abide forever. For the Lord loves justice and does not forsake His godly ones; they are preserved forever, but the descendants of the wicked will be cut off. The righteous will inherit the land and dwell in it forever. The mouth of the righteous utters wisdom, and his tongue speaks justice. The law of his God is in his heart; His steps do not slip. The wicked spies upon the righteous and seeks to kill him. The Lord will not leave him in his hand or let him be condemned when he is judged. Wait for the Lord and keep His way, and He will exalt you to inherit the land; when the wicked are cut off, you will see it. I have seen a wicked, violent man spreading himself like a luxuriant tree in its native soil. Then he passed

away, and lo, he was no more; I sought for him, but he could not be found. Mark the blameless man, and behold the upright; for the man of peace will have a posterity. But transgressors will be altogether destroyed; The posterity of the wicked will be cut off. But the salvation of the righteous is from the Lord; He is their strength in time of trouble. The Lord helps them and delivers them; He delivers them from the wicked and saves them, because they take refuge in Him.
Psalm 37

~

There is so much to glean from this passage. One of the main themes is "Do not fret". Don't worry about what might happen because you are only borrowing trouble. Even if it is a possibility, we should not think about it until it is a certainty. There is something to be said for being prepared, but don't let it trouble you, don't dwell on it. Leave it in God's hands to be concerned about it, for He is the only One who can do anything about it. Worry will not change anything. Rest and wait patiently for Him, have peace in the knowledge that God is in control, knowing that He works all for your benefit. "Trust God and do good" is twofold, but they go together. Basically, trust God to take care of, provide for and protect you, and continue walking in His ways leaving the future (and the past) to Him. This is the follow up to "do not fret." And part of that is committing your way to God, that is, giving Him control of your life, obeying His commands, and trusting Him to take care of you. "Delight yourself in the Lord and He will give you the desire of your heart" is also twofold. What it boils down to is that if you are truly delighting in God, then you will have the desire of your heart, which *is* God, and everything He gives you will be seen as an added blessing. It is not a vending machine where you put something in and get what you want back out. Delight in God is the key to true contentment. God sustains the righteous. He protects those who trust and follow Him. Rest in the knowledge that you have a permanent inheritance with Him. He has planned your life. He will take care of you because He knows what will happen. He blesses obedience and righteousness. As long as we stay true to Him, He will be faithful to us. It is from God that we get our salvation and He provides our strength. He helps and delivers us because we take refuge in Him. So go to Him and have peace and rest, for He will not disappoint.

How blessed is he whose transgression is forgiven, whose sin is covered! How blessed is the man to whom the Lord does not impute iniquity, and in whose spirit there is no deceit! When I kept silent about my sin, my body wasted away through my groaning all day long. For day and night Your hand was heavy upon me; my vitality was drained away as with the fever heat of summer. Selah. I acknowledged my sin to You, and my iniquity I did not hide; I said, "I will confess my transgressions to the Lord"; and You forgave the guilt of my sin. Selah. Therefore, let everyone who is godly pray to You in a time when You may be found; surely in a flood of great waters they will not reach him. You are my hiding place; You preserve me from trouble; You surround me with songs of deliverance. Selah. I will instruct you and teach you in the way which you should go; I will counsel you with My eye upon you. Do not be as the horse or as the mule which have no understanding, whose trappings include bit and bridle to hold them in check, otherwise they will not come near to you. Many are the sorrows of the wicked, but he who trusts in the Lord, lovingkindness shall surround him. Be glad in the Lord and rejoice, you righteous ones; and shout for joy, all you who are upright in heart.
Psalm 32

~

Keeping silent about what we have done may save us embarrassment, but it is like cancer which eats from the inside. As with poisonous fumes, the only way to be freed from them is to open the doors and let it out. <u>Confession is the first step</u> to healing and renewal. This is also true for victims of abuse. Though you have done nothing wrong, you remain a prisoner to your pain until you release it by telling God and by telling someone who can help you and encourage you. It seems counter intuitive, but that is how God works. We were made to need others. <u>The second step is forgiveness.</u> It does not say God forgave me because of this or because I did that. It just says that God forgave. He has promised to forgive, all you have to do is ask. This also means that you need to forgive, as He forgave you. Forgiveness doesn't excuse what has been done; it doesn't release them from punishment. What it does is release *you* from the pain, from the emotional hold they have on you. <u>Therefore, let everyone pray</u>! It is a surety, so don't hold back. Talk to God about everything. <u>Make God your hiding place</u>; don't hide from Him. He is the only place where true healing can be found, and He will protect you if you go to Him. There is no sin too great that He would turn you away. He will deliver you from your past, from your sin, from your pain. He will then become your guide and teacher. He will help you avoid trouble and sin. Willingly trust in Him and submit to His will for your life so that His loving kindness will envelope you. Allow yourself to delight in Him. Be happy because He loves you, because He has given you grace and mercy, because He has saved you. Be blessed!

And He has said to me, "My grace is sufficient for you, for power is perfected in weakness." Most gladly, therefore, I will rather boast about my weaknesses, so that the power of Christ may dwell in me.
2 Corinthians 12:9

~

How is it that power is perfected in weakness? It is because when we are weak we trust more in God. We have to, so His power has more control over our lives. It is in our weakness that we realize we need His power. The more we trust in Him, the more opportunity His power has to work. It is by His grace that we are saved and healed. It is all we need in our imperfection. We cannot heal ourselves, earn our salvation or His delight or reward, or find healing, salvation or blessing elsewhere. It is only by His grace. In our weakness we become aware of our insufficiency and our need for His grace. That is why Paul boasted, or gloried, in his weakness, because that is when the power of Christ was most active in him. When you feel like you are not good enough, like you just can't possibly go on any longer, like you are too distant from God, remember that this is where your strength lies; in the realization of where you truly are, powerless and in need. Turn to the power of the cross. Trust in Christ to carry you, to heal you, to perfect you, and He will do it.

Ask and it will be given to you, seek and you will find, knock and it will be opened to you. For everyone who asks receives, and he who seeks finds, and to him who knocks it will be opened. Or what man among you who, when his son asks for a loaf, will give him a stone? Or if he asks for a fish, he will not give him a snake, will he? If you then, being evil, know how to give good gifts to your children, how much more will your Father in heaven give what is good to those who ask Him!
Matthew 7:7-11

~

Have you asked God for what you want and need? Have you asked with the faith that He will give it to you? We do need to be careful to not assume that if we ask and believe that it will be done regardless, because that may not be God's will for us. And not receiving what you ask for is no reflection of your level of faith, but do you trust God to provide? Do you believe that He is a kind and gracious Father who wants to bless and give you good gifts? Do you believe that He is not only capable of doing what you need, but that He will? Do not let your experience with any person taint your view of God. He is perfect and while we are images or reflections of God to some extent, the bad in us is a reflection of Satan and we need to see that differentiation. The bad we see or experience in others is no reflection of God. God can do no evil; He is incapable of wrong or cruel thoughts or actions. Believe that He is good and kind. Believe that He loves you. Believe that He wants to bless you. Believe that He will do good in your life. And trust Him to do it.

Consider it all joy, my brethren, when you encounter various trials, knowing that the testing of your faith produces endurance. And let endurance have its perfect result, so that you may be perfect and complete, lacking in nothing.
James 1:2-4

~

There is a difference between joy and happiness. Joy is not dependant on situation or circumstance. Joy is having your hope and identity set in Christ so that no matter what happens, you can have peace knowing who you are, Whose you are, and where you are going. It is knowing that God has everything under control, so you don't have to worry or be upset or afraid because of what is going on. We are supposed to have joy in every situation, because those situations are really for our benefit. We know because of this verse that the trials we go through will improve our faith and our character. They are the refining fire that makes us stronger and more pure. With each trial we become stronger in God and more pure and complete, **if** we respond with joy instead of grumbling, complaining or self pity. If we respond to trials in a godly way, trusting in God, then it will produce godly fruit in our lives. If we don't then we will be miserable. Focus your hope on Christ. Intend to be joyful and to use this hard time to benefit you, and maybe even others. Look for what you can learn from what you are going through so that something good can come out of it. Finish well.

> *Be anxious for nothing, but in everything by prayer and supplication with thanksgiving let your requests be made known to God. And the peace of God, which surpasses all comprehension, will guard your hearts and minds in Christ Jesus.*
> *Philippians 4:6-7*

~

<u>Do not worry about anything</u>. This is a pointed command that is followed by a substitute. Instead of worry, <u>pray to God</u>; tell Him your grief and praise Him. He doesn't just say don't worry and leave it at that. He tells you what to do instead of worrying: give it to Him. Entrust Him with your fears and troubles and then let Him take care of them. One important part to note is to do it <u>with thanksgiving</u>. This changes our attitude from fear (which shows a lack of trust in God and His ability and willingness to help us) and possibly grumbling to one of gratitude, which shows dependence and trust in God. Also, praise is one of our most powerful weapons. God inhabits our praise, and if He is "inhabiting" us, then Satan is expelled. When we are praising God, Satan is bound and paralyzed. His ability to lie to us and make us doubt God is incapacitated. There is a promise that follows the command: <u>if you place your worry and trust in God, His peace (which is so great we couldn't even imagine it) will guard our hearts and minds.</u> Against what? More doubt and fear. If we stay focused on God with praise and thanksgiving, and entrust Him with our fears, He will protect us from becoming bogged down with worry and fear again. If we are focusing on Him, no bad thought can enter our minds. It's like a force field; as long as we stay inside the force field, we can't be hit by Satan's arrows of fear, but as soon as we remove ourselves from God, and stop trusting Him, we will be vulnerable to fear, worry and doubt again. Stay in the force field! Trust God and allow His peace to envelope you.

> *Finally, brethren, whatever is true, whatever is honorable, whatever is right, whatever if pure, whatever is lovely, whatever is of good repute, if there is any excellence and if anything worthy of praise, ponder these things.*
> *Philippians 4:8*

~

How many times do our fears, doubts and anxiety come from thinking about something that *may* happen in the future? How often do the things others say or do hurt us even more because we dwell on them and allow them to damage us? Our thoughts play a huge role in our emotions. If we are thinking about things that are hurtful, we feel hurt, but if we think about things that are happy, we feel happy. We have another command here: to "ponder" the things listed in this verse. God is giving us a list of things that are to occupy our thoughts. First they should be <u>true</u>. If you are thinking about something that is false (or may not have happened yet) stop. It will make you unhappy. It should also be <u>honorable</u>, or worthy of respect; holy versus profane, corrupt or vulgar. It should be <u>right</u>, or aligned with God's principles and standard of holiness. It should be <u>pure</u>, or morally clean. Ephesians 5:11-12 says that some deeds are a sin even to mention because that contact is corrupting. If it is sin to talk about them, then we should not think about them either. What is in our minds is in our hearts and our hearts are supposed to be pure. Our thoughts should also be focused on things that are <u>lovely</u>, or literally advantageous to love, pleasing, kind, gracious. Think about the fruit of the spirit. It should also be of <u>good repute</u>, going back to that verse in Ephesians. We shouldn't think about things that are dishonorable. Whatever is of <u>excellence (virtue) or worthy of praise</u> are things that we should be thinking about. If we focus our thoughts on God, and the things of God, how can we be sad or hurt? Think about that and let Him take care of evil.

Rejoice always; pray without ceasing; in everything give thanks; for this is God's will for you in Christ Jesus.
1 Thessalonians 5:16-18

~

Here again, we have these commands. <u>Rejoice always</u>. We should always have an attitude of joy. Even in times of trouble, we should be joyful. This doesn't necessarily mean to be happy about our circumstances, but content that we are in God's hands regardless of what happens. Delight in what you do have, namely God's salvation, love and grace. <u>Pray without ceasing</u>. This doesn't mean that you are physically on your knees 24/7, but rather praying persistently and regularly, keeping that communication line to God open. Especially if you are in trials, it is beneficial to always bring your heart and needs before God. It helps you to keep focus where you should, on God. Additionally, it helps foster an attitude of dependence on God and transfers your trust to Him. If you develop that habit when times are good, it will be easier and more natural when times are hard. <u>In everything, give thanks.</u> We need to always have an attitude of gratefulness. Even if times are really bad, God has still given you life and salvation, which is eternal life. You may have sorrow on earth, but you will spend the rest of eternity in joyous rapture. Is that not worth being grateful for? <u>For this is God's will for you</u>. That is talking not only about your situation but those commands. He wants these commands for you because He knows they will make you happier with life, being joyful, in communion with Him and grateful to Him. All of these will help lift your spirits. He knows that, which is why He wants you to do them. Follow His lead and accept the blessings that come from joyful obedience.

Unless the LORD builds the house, they labor in vain who build it; unless the LORD guards the city, the watchman keeps awake in vain.
Psalm 127:1

~

God can do anything. None can defeat Him. Our enemies will not prevail. If there is something God doesn't want to happen, it won't. If we are not on His side, we will not succeed. We must trust in Him and follow Him in order to conquer, because ultimately He is the Victor and there is no victory without Him. Trying to fight temptation on our own produces failure. Even if what we are doing is good, if we are trying to do it on our own, or if our motives are wrong, God will not help us and we will not succeed. It must be God who does the work through us. We must be the tool, not the power source. We must allow God to use us for His glory, resisting the temptation to do it on our own. Healing can come, but it must come from God. Allow God to have control of your life and circumstances; otherwise, you labor in vain.

Praise the Lord! Praise the Lord from the heavens; praise Him in the heights! Praise Him, all His angels; praise Him, all His hosts! Praise Him, sun and moon; praise Him, all stars of light! Praise Him, highest heavens, and the waters that are above the heavens! Let them praise the name of the Lord, for He commanded and they were created. He has also established them forever and ever; He has made a decree which will not pass away. Praise the Lord from the earth, sea monsters and all deeps; fire and hail, snow and clouds; stormy wind, fulfilling His word; mountains and all hills; fruit trees and all cedars; beasts and all cattle; creeping things and winged fowl; kings of the earth and all peoples; princes and all judges of the earth; both young men and virgins; old men and children. Let them praise the name of the Lord, for His name alone is exalted; His glory is above earth and heaven. And He has lifted up a horn for His people, praise for all His godly ones; even for the sons of Israel, a people near to Him.
Praise the Lord!
Psalm 148

~

God is the most supreme, powerful, mighty, wonderful Being we could ever encounter. He created everything in existence, and yet with all His power, He is also completely loving and full of grace and mercy. He is just and good. He is the only one worthy, and we are commanded to praise Him. Praise exalts Him, shows others what we think of Him, glorifies and beautifies Him, but it also blesses us.

We receive blessing when we give God His due because we are in line with the way things are meant to be. That order naturally creates blessing. It blesses us because we are allowing God His proper place in our lives. He is worthy to be praised. Spend some time praising God for who He is and what He has done. Let that blessing of humility fall on your life.

Give thanks to the Lord, for He is good, for His lovingkindness is everlasting. Give thanks to the God of gods, for His lovingkindness is everlasting. Give thanks to the Lord of lords, for His lovingkindness is everlasting. To Him who alone does great wonders, for His lovingkindness is everlasting; to Him who made the heavens with skill, for His lovingkindness is everlasting; to Him who spread out the earth above the waters, for His lovingkindness is everlasting; to Him who made the great lights, for His lovingkindness is everlasting: the sun to rule by day, for His lovingkindness is everlasting, the moon and stars to rule by night, for His lovingkindness is everlasting. To Him who smote the Egyptians in their firstborn, for His lovingkindness is everlasting, and brought Israel out from their midst, for His lovingkindness is everlasting, with a strong hand and an outstretched arm, for His lovingkindness is everlasting. To Him who divided the Red Sea asunder, for His lovingkindness is everlasting, and made Israel pass through the midst of it, for His lovingkindness is everlasting; but He overthrew Pharaoh and his army in the Red Sea, for His lovingkindness is everlasting. To Him who led His people through the wilderness, for His lovingkindness is everlasting; to Him who smote great kings, for His lovingkindness is everlasting, and slew mighty kings, for His lovingkindness is everlasting: Sihon, king of the Amorites, for His

> lovingkindness is everlasting, and Og, king of Bashan, for His lovingkindness is everlasting, and gave their land as a heritage, for His lovingkindness is everlasting, even a heritage to Israel His servant, for His lovingkindness is everlasting. Who remembered us in our low estate, for His lovingkindness is everlasting, and has rescued us from our adversaries, for His lovingkindness is everlasting; Who gives food to all flesh, for His lovingkindness is everlasting. Give thanks to the God of heaven, for His lovingkindness is everlasting.
> Psalm 136

~

In the midst of hard times, it is difficult to think of anything else. When the pain of what you are going through is all that you can feel, it is hard to comprehend life outside of it. But remember that God is always loving. That is important to remember. That is why the author repeats it every other line. God did all of these amazing miracles, but all of that just proves that He is love. Take some time to list a few things that God has done for you. They may be small, like seeing a beautiful rainbow, a kind word from a stranger, a smile from a child, but they are still blessings. Focus on what God has done, remember His love and let that carry you through your season of pain.

I know how to get along with humble means, and I also know how to live in prosperity; in any and every circumstance I have learned the secret of being filled and going hungry, both of having abundance and suffering need. I can do all things through Him who strengthens me.
Philippians 4:12-13

~

Paul had learned the secret to life regardless of circumstance. He had learned to be content with whatever he had because God is the One who provides and sustains. He depended on God's strength and provision and was never upset or sad about having little, nor prideful or ungrateful about having much. He was joyful in all situations because he relied on God and not on what he had. Because he relied on God, he had the strength to withstand anything and everything. If he had relied on himself or someone else, he would have been stressed and disappointed, but God does not disappoint. Have you been relying on yourself or someone else to provide for you, whether for physical, emotional or even spiritual needs? Do you wonder why you are not happy with the results? It is because God is the One who provides. He is the One we should go to for everything, first and not as a last resource. He is ultimately the One in control, no matter how much we try to control our lives. Are you lacking? Go to God. Find your contentment in Him.

> *And the LORD will continually guide you, and satisfy your desire in scorched places, and give strength to your bones; and you will be like a watered garden, and like a spring of water whose waters do not fail.*
> Isaiah 58:11

In this passage, God had been talking about the fake religion of Israel. They fasted and sacrificed so they would appear pious, when really those acts were supposed to glorify God. The purpose of our "religion" is to glorify God and help others, not promote or benefit ourselves. If we are faithful to God as we should be, then the promise of this verse will follow. God will guide you, satisfy you and give you strength. Then you will be like a fountain that is never dry. Have you been serving God and serving others out of love lately? It is difficult to focus outside of your problems when times are hard, but maybe that is the key to getting through or out of it: helping others. Make a meal for an elderly neighbor, watch a single mom's kids so she can get groceries, bring hot coffee to construction workers in the snow. Blessing others will bless you as well, and there is no better cure for depression or the blues than helping another person, even and especially when they can give nothing in return.

For God has not given us a spirit of timidity, but of power and love and discipline.
2 Timothy 1:7
~

God made us, and He did not intend for us to be fearful. Timidity, insecurity and fear are all from Satan. They are weapons he uses to control us. We must trust God to take care of us rather than be afraid or worried about what will happen. Trust that He knew what He was doing when He made you. Be confident in who He made you to be. He made you to have His power so that you can use it for Him and against Satan. He made you to be loving as He is loving because He has given you His love. He made you to have sound judgment (mind) and self control. He never intended for us to be controlled by fear, substances, emotions or other people. We need to stand strong in God and who He made us to be. Get rid of your fear and trust God and the power and love that He has given you.

Stories of Suffering

"The people of the Bible didn't know the outcome of their own stories any more than we do."

Unknown

Sarah
Genesis 12, 15, 16, 18, 20, 21
~

Sarah was Abraham's wife. She had traveled everywhere with him. They never really settled down for very long in one place. Twice in their journeys, they came to a new place and Abraham was afraid that the king would kill him to take Sarah, so he lied and told them she was his sister (a half truth) and let them take her so that he could live. Both times she was saved by God and returned to him, but I'm sure she didn't appreciate the cowardice of her husband. They were childless and eventually gave up hope of having a son and heir. Even though God promised (when Abraham was 75) that they would, 25 years passed before that promise came about. Long before that happened, Sarah became impatient and decided to make the promise happen. She took one of her slave girls, Hagar, and gave her to Abraham to have a child for her. The plan worked, but it also backfired. Hagar (the slave) despised Sarah because she succeeded in having a son when Sarah could not. Sarah blamed Abraham for this (no doubt also because she was jealous of the young woman her husband slept with). Abraham weakly told Sarah to do what she wanted, so she abused Hagar. Fast forward thirteen years. God again told Abraham that he would have a legitimate heir through Sarah. Sarah did not believe the angel who brought this news. She was, by now, 90 and Abraham 100. But the miracle happened and she had a son, Isaac, who became the father of Israel.

Sarah went through many hardships. She was a nomad, wife of a weak and unfaithful husband, despised by her slave because she could not have children. She was forced to wait many years to have the baby that she was promised, and she did not always react in a godly way. Some of her suffering was her own fault. If she had trusted God to fulfill His promise, she would not have had trouble with Hagar, and subsequently Hagar's descendants, through her son

Ishmael, became Israel's enemies. Centuries of pain and war came about because one woman did not trust God. Learn from her example, not to be like her, but to learn from her mistakes. Don't give up on God to do what He has promised, to provide for you, or to change or save someone. Many are divorced because they gave up on God to work in their marriages. Don't leave that kind of legacy. 1 Peter 3:1-6 is the kind of legacy you want to leave, one that brings honor to you, your family, and to God.

Joseph
Genesis 37, 39-47
~

Joseph was the eleventh of twelve sons of Jacob, yet he was his father's favorite. His brothers were jealous of their father's love for Joseph, so they planned to kill him. Their oldest brother talked them out of it, but before he could rescue Joseph, the others sold him to slave traders. He was sold again in Egypt, and spent many years as a slave of Potiphar. His integrity was so great that he was promoted to head of all Potiphar's house. His master's wife tried to seduce him and he fled, so she lied and told Potiphar that he had attacked her. Joseph was sent to prison for a crime he did not commit. No doubt, as a Hebrew slave in Egypt, there wasn't even a trial, but again his integrity was such that the warden gave him some form of authority in the prison. After several years in prison, two inmates had dreams on the same night. Joseph interpreted them, and they came true three days later. But those inmates forgot about him. Some time later, Pharaoh had dreams that none of his wise men could interpret. Then one of the inmates (who had been released just as Joseph had prophesied from his dream) mentioned Joseph to Pharaoh. Joseph was summoned, interpreted the dream, and gave wise counsel to Pharaoh, yet through it all he gave glory for those miracles to God. Pharaoh was so impressed that he made Joseph second over the whole country and put him in charge of preparing for the famine foretold by his dreams. In the middle of the famine, Joseph's brothers came to get food from Egypt, but they didn't recognize Joseph when they saw him. On their second trip, he discovered that they had had a change of heart over those many years, and treated their youngest brother with love, instead of the jealousy they had for Joseph. He then revealed himself, forgave them, and brought the whole clan to live with him. The brothers were still afraid that he would seek revenge, but he replied, "It is over. What you meant for evil, God meant for good."

Even though Joseph's brothers were trying to hurt him and do evil, God made it all work out to help everyone. Joseph could have despaired and grumbled over his poor and unjust treatment, but he didn't. He trusted God's sovereignty and goodness. He didn't let the bad events and people make him bitter. He maintained his integrity and honored God. Through his humility, God made him one of the most important men in the world at that time, but that wouldn't have happened if he hadn't been humble and open to God's teaching. The trials he went through refined his character and gave him the wisdom, strength and trust in God that he would need to rule later on. He didn't know what God's plan was, but he trusted it nonetheless. Follow Joseph's example, don't let bad circumstances and bad people influence you. Stay strong in the Lord, be true to Him and trust in His plan and faithfulness.

Exodus 16

~

Before this chapter, God had sent Moses to bring Israel out of Egypt. He had done many miracles and signs before Pharaoh. He had just parted the Red Sea, destroyed the Egyptian army, and provided water for them out of a rock. Obviously, He is a mighty God of power. However, when they got to the wilderness, instead of asking God for food, or waiting for Him to provide, they immediately started to complain, insinuating that God meant to kill them by starvation and talked about how wrongly they were being treated. How quick they were to forget what God had already done for them. They were not grateful for any of it, but soaked it up and looked for more like selfish children. That is the first of many lessons in the chapter. God provides for our needs, but we need to ask and be grateful for what we already have. Their unhappiness was of their own making, because they were selfish and not content with what they had. They didn't trust in God's goodness, that He really did love them and have their best in mind. They had spent too much time among the pagan gods that were greedy, selfish and cruel. Ours is a good God, not like others. He had enduring patience with them. They also needed to learn to obey Him. God's rules are not designed for torture or out of desire for mastery, nor are they mere suggestions that we can take or leave as we choose. They have a purpose, a good purpose. If the Israelites had trusted God, they would have seen that. God did not provide for them immediately because He wanted to humble them, to remind them of their place and His. They needed to put Him first in their lives. When God did provide for them, they were commanded to "come near before the Lord," because He heard their complaints. They distanced themselves from Him because they were unhappy with Him, but if they had come close to God to begin with, they would have seen His love and kindness. They would have learned to trust Him and to come to Him with their needs rather than trying to run away. When God provided, everyone gathered as much as they needed. No one had excess and no one came short; there was exactly enough. God knows what we need and will provide it if we trust Him, if we ask Him. So draw near, come close to God. Let Him know what you need, but also get to know Him, learn to trust Him. Taste and see that He is good.

Psalm 105

~

It is important for us to remember the good things that God has done. We should always be thinking about how He has helped us and others. This positive focus helps to keep us from depression, despair and bitterness. It also glorifies God. God is faithful. Though it took hundreds of years for fulfillment, He kept His promise to Abraham. He protected Isaac and Jacob. He placed Joseph in a strategic position to help his family during the famine. Then, when the people had forgotten God, He allowed Pharaoh to make them slaves so that they would want to leave Egypt and return to the land God had promised them. He prepared Moses to deliver them and sent the plagues so that the Egyptians would want the Jews to leave. When they left, the Egyptians were so happy to get rid of them that they let the Jews take treasure from there. God guided and protected them as they traveled. He miraculously provided them with food and water in the desert.

Look at God's divine plan in all of this. Look at how it came about over the course of centuries. The Israelites wanted to (and some did) complain and felt like they had been abandoned and treated poorly. They couldn't see God's plan. If they had trusted God, that He is good and sovereign and working on their behalf, they wouldn't have been so unhappy. There are many reasons to praise God. These are just a few of them. Have you been upset because of the bad things happening in your life? Do you feel abandoned or abused by God? Remember these truths. Believe them and trust God to work for you. Find something to praise Him for today and share it with someone.

Ruth

Ruth was a pagan foreigner who married a Jew living in her country, but her husband died and she was left alone with no children. Rather than go back to her people, Ruth remained faithful to the God and mother of her husband. She left all that she knew in the midst of her sorrow. When Ruth and her mother-in-law returned to her husband's hometown, she worked hard in the fields to glean food. She was surely looked down upon as a foreigner and avoided by most in the town. It is possible that losing her husband and having no children was seen as judgment from God for something. Nevertheless, Ruth remained strong, willing and kind. She didn't let all of this get her down or embitter her. In the end, she married a gracious, wealthy man who loved her, and she ended up being in the lineage of Christ. Ruth never knew the great plan God had for her life or her family, to bring about the salvation of the world, but she remained faithful anyway.

An interesting thing to note is that Ruth chose part of her suffering. She chose to leave her people, home and religion in order to go with her mother-in-law even though she knew it would be difficult and she would face a lot of hardship. Why would someone choose to leave everything they knew in that kind of situation? Partly it was out of devotion to her mother-in-law, but it was also partly because she chose faith in her husband's God rather than the false religions of her home land. Ruth chose to serve God even though she knew she would suffer as a result. And she was blessed beyond her imagination for her faithfulness. Suffering is not something that we should always run from. Sometimes it is the best thing that could happen to us.

Hannah
1 Samuel 1, 2

~

Hannah was a Hebrew woman, but one of two wives of her husband. The other wife had many children, which was a sign of honor and favor from God. Hannah had none, but the Bible says that her husband loved her greatly. It didn't bother him that she was barren. He gave her extra portions of everything, but the other wife teased her. Finally, one year as they went to Shiloh for the annual feast, she was so distressed that she prayed earnestly to God about it, alone at the temple. She made a vow to God that if she conceived a son, she would dedicate him to serve God at the temple. The high priest thought that she was drunk because he could not hear what she was saying and rebuked her, but she explained the situation to him and he blessed her. After they went home, Hannah conceived a son and named him Samuel. About 3 years later when he was weaned, she kept her vow to God and brought him to the temple to serve. Every year she would bring him gifts when they came, but she did not raise him after that. Samuel eventually took over for the priest, Eli, an honor usually reserved for the priest's sons. He became one of the most famous prophets of Israel. God also blessed Hannah's faithfulness by causing her to conceive five more children.

Hannah could have remained depressed and upset over her situation. She could have become hard and bitter. Instead, she turned to God with her sorrow and distress. God blessed her faith, and she honored God by keeping her vow. It had to be incredibly difficult to leave her only child like that, especially when he was so young. It would have been tempting to keep him and forsake her vow once she had her child, but she was faithful to God, and He blessed her even more for it. Take courage from Hannah's story. Trust God. It may take years for your promise to come through. Keep hoping in God. The Bible says that those who are faithful with the little they are given will be trusted with more. Don't be proven faithless and prevent God's blessing. Be true to God, trust in Him, and don't give up hope.

Habakkuk

~

Habakkuk was a prophet directly before Israel was sent into captivity and exile. He watched as God seemingly stood by while nation after nation abused Israel. The first chapter talks about what happened, and Habbakuk's despair and disappointment. The second chapter is God's answer to his questioning. Chapter three records his repentance and restoration of trust in God. He praises God for His majesty and sovereignty. <u>Read these now.</u> No matter what happens in life, we should never give up on or accuse God. He is good and faithful, and He cannot be otherwise. Pour out your heart to Him. Tell him your troubles. Let Him take care of your problems and trust in His plan, even if you don't know what it is. Let your days and your prayers end as this book, with praise, hope and trust.

Esther
~

Esther was a Jewish girl born after the Jews had been taken captive first by Babylon, then by Persia. Her parents had died and she was raised by an older cousin. Her life was far from easy. Though she and her family were not slaves, they were exiles, and she was an orphan. She was taken from her home to be groomed in the king's palace as a possible candidate for the next queen. She hid her true identity and chose a new name because of the hostile, anti-Semitic views of some of the top officials. Even though she was chosen to become queen, when one of the king's advisers devised a scheme to kill all of the Jews, she wasn't safe from that threat. Esther endured a lot of persecution and hardship. If we left the story here, it would be pretty depressing, but it continues.

As the queen, she had influence with the king and was able to persuade him to rescue her people. Everything Esther went through was finally made clear in God's ultimate plan. It was all for a reason. She could not have known until the end why she had to go through all of those hardships, but she remained faithful to God. She did not whine or complain, rather she pressed on. God was able to use Esther in His great plan because she was honorable and faithful. She chose to be led by the wisdom of the Spirit instead of her emotions. Be encouraged by her story. Maybe the plans God has for you aren't as grand as saving an entire nation in one stroke, but He does have a plan for you. Stay faithful. Allow God to use you for His purpose. You never know what might come!

Nehemiah 4

~

Some of the Israelites had returned to Jerusalem after their exile and were trying to rebuild the city. There were many in the area determined to keep them from it, intimidating them by casting doubt and threatening to attack. The Israelites had to work in shifts with half of the people armed and standing guard in case the enemy attacked while those working kept weapons close at hand. They were frightened, for they were not soldiers and outnumbered, but they kept working and finished the wall in record time.

There are many times in life when we meet with discouragements or fear. The enemy uses many circumstances to keep us afraid, weak and defeated. Sometimes we may face what seem to be insurmountable odds or hopeless trials. We may see no hope or end to our difficulty, no way through or around it. But we are not the ones the surety rests upon. Our hope is God. He has the power; He has the strength. He knows what is happening and also what will happen. You are not alone. You are not even in charge! God is there and He is your guide. Follow Him. He knows how to get you through and He will not leave you. Verse 20 says "our God will fight for us." And He will. He will lead you and fight for you, and He never loses. Turn to Him for help, guidance, and comfort. Trust Him to carry you through this time.

The Blind Man
John 9

~

In this chapter of John, Jesus heals a man who had been born blind. This story is a great example of when trials are not a result of anyone's sin. It is so easy to look at someone struggling and write it off as punishment for some particular sin, but we are not God. We do not know nor should we try to judge the reason, as Christ clearly explains here. Whatever physically made this man blind, the purpose was to glorify God. Surely the man did not know the reason for his infirmity as he had spent his whole life blind. God will tell us the reason, if we have to know, when we need to know it and not before. Now this man went from being a social outcast to a direct vessel chosen to manifest God's glory! How cool is that? Would that not have made up for the lifetime of hardship? We too can be vessels to manifest the glory of God. We do this by glorifying God, praising Him in the midst of our trials, and thanking Him no matter the circumstance. This transfers attention from us to God. It also changes our posture from one of pity to praise, which glorifies God (and is a manifestation of it) in itself. We also need to give glory to God when our trials are ended. Even if our physical infirmity is medically cured, it is still by the grace of God that you received the cure. As this man did, we need to remain constant in our praise and affirmation of God. God knows the reason for what we are going through, whether we do or not. Remain faithful to Him, trust in Him, be a manifestation of His glory.

Jesus
Mark 15
~

Jesus is, without a doubt, the person least deserving to suffer in history. He is perfect; He has never done anything wrong. He is God's beloved Son. While on earth He served God selflessly, but He suffered cruelly. Sadly, He was denied and abandoned by all of His companions. He was falsely accused of crimes and condemned by the very crowds He served and healed. He was beaten by the Romans almost beyond physical recognition with whips that had metal tips, a scourging that many did not survive. Then the Romans made fun of Him, dressing Him as a king and pretending to worship Him. They made a crown with long thorns that they beat onto His head with sticks. By this time His blood had started to stick to the robes they put on Him and they ripped them off, making the bleeding even worse. They made Him walk to the top of the hill outside of town to be crucified. They hammered nails through His wrists and feet, and hung Him by those nails, naked, before the whole city. Above all this, He was abandoned by God as He took on the sins of the whole world, to be our sacrifice for the bad things we have done, to pay the penalty that we owe. He endured what we deserved. But through it all, He loved and forgave those who did it. He willingly died on the cross and rose again so that we could be saved. It was the epitome of suffering, and of love. Will you accept His love and the sacrifice that He made for you? Will you follow His example through your suffering?

Paul
2 Corinthians 11:21-33
~

Here, Paul chronicles all the hardships that he endured during his missions. He was imprisoned many times. He was beaten more times than he could count, often close to death; five times he was whipped by the Jews with the maximum allowable, thirty nine lashes. Three times the Romans beat him with rods. He was even stoned once, and left for dead, but God revived him. He was shipwrecked three times, one of those times in the water for twenty four hours. He traveled a lot, encountering danger from robbers and river crossings, mobs and wild animals, drowning and betrayal. He worked very hard, lost a lot of sleep, went without food and water, and was exposed to the elements at times. He endured those things **while** he was doing God's work. Added to all this was the great burden in his heart for God's church. You would think that God would protect him in order to help the ministry. At the beginning of the passage he says that he had just as much call as any other person to expect good treatment, yet he endured so much more. He wasn't complaining, but showing that Christians suffer, that we have no reason to boast about ourselves, and that our suffering is to magnify God's glory.

Maybe you think that you do not deserve to be treated the way you have been, to go through your circumstances. Are you a better person than the apostle Paul? Have you done more in service to God than he? Have you been more faithful and pure? Jesus promised that we would suffer. Jesus Himself suffered. What in you could cause you to deserve better treatment? What matters is not what we go through, but how we respond to it. Will we be like Paul and glorify God, counting ourselves lucky to suffer for Him? Or will we wallow in self pity and grumble against God? We were made children of God while we were still His enemies. He paid our ransom and redeemed us even though we could never deserve or earn it. All the bad we go through is nothing compared to the punishment that we deserve. We don't deserve anything good. Praise the One who took your punishment and has given you so many blessings!

Corrie Ten Boom
The Hiding Place
~

Corrie grew up in Holland, born in the late 1800's. As a young woman, she and a young man fell in love, but he would not marry her because she was the daughter of a poor working man. She never married her whole life; instead, she lived at home with her sister and father. In the 1930's, when the Nazi's began to eradicate the world of Jews, Corrie and several family members joined a network to smuggle Jews out of Europe. They did this successfully for many years, but they were eventually caught. She and her sister were separated from their elderly father who died shortly after. They were taken to a concentration camp where they were humiliated, beaten, starved, and overworked, but through it all they remained faithful to God. They managed to smuggle a Bible into the camp and led Bible studies and prayer groups, encouraging the other women. Before the end of the war, Corrie's sister died from malnutrition and disease, and Corrie was left alone like so many other women there who had lost husbands, children and families. Some became bitter and cursed God because of how they had been treated, but Corrie did not. Ironically, she was eventually released for the purpose of showing the world that the Nazis weren't cruel. Years later, while speaking at a conference, Corrie met one of the Nazi guards who had been at the camp with her. Facing one of the men who had caused so much suffering in her life, she encountered an even more difficult choice. He asked her to forgive him. Anyone would have understood her desire to hold him in judgment, to not let him off, but she didn't. She forgave him and in turn freed herself from a life of pain. She knew that what he did, even against her, was between him and God, and what she did was between her and God. She obeyed God's command to love and forgive all, and enjoyed the blessings of that obedience. She did not let her circumstances make her turn against God.

Are you holding a grudge? Has someone hurt you or betrayed you in a horrible way? Maybe you have done something and you cannot get away from the shame and guilt. God has already forgiven you or that person who hurt you. Are you above God that you should hold onto something that He has already taken care of? Remember that God is also just. He repays wrong-doing in one way or another. Let Him take care of it. Let go of the pain. Forgive, and accept His forgiveness. Do not stay in bondage to the sin and pain.

Horatio G. Spafford
www.spaffordcenter.org

~

Horatio lived in America during the mid 1800's. He was a prosperous lawyer near Chicago and had a growing family of four daughters. During the great Chicago fire, he and his wife worked tirelessly to help refugees. Later, they took a vacation to Europe to recuperate from the work. Last minute business delayed his departure, but he talked his family into going on ahead of him. In the middle of the Atlantic crossing, due to heavy fog, their ship collided with another and sank so quickly that only twenty seven people were rescued out of hundreds. His wife was one of the survivors and sent him a telegraph simply stating "saved alone". He left immediately to join her. As his ship crossed the place where his daughters perished, he penned these lines…

> When peace like a river attendeth my way
> When sorrows like sea billows roll
> Whatever my lot, Thou hast taught me to say
> It is well, it is well with my soul.[vii]

They were later blessed with another daughter and a son, but their son died of scarlet fever when he was young. Through it all they never gave up on their faith. In the midst of their suffering, they continued to serve God and others. They moved to Jerusalem (shortly after another daughter was born) and started a "colony" to minister to Jews and Arabs alike that flourished even through the World Wars. They remained faithful to God, even through continued hardship and sorrow. Let God teach you, as He did them, to say in any circumstance, "It is well with my soul."

Hope In Suffering

The ache of sorrow deeply held
Wanting what is lost forever
Dreams ended before they can begin
Shadow every view and endeavor

Hollow pain permeates every thought
Reality so vague yet so firm
Truth intangibly real
Valid for a never-ending term

Though pain from the sharp dagger of death
Becomes gradually more numb
It returns repeatedly for another jab
While a reminder of what has come

One pain replaces another
As the sharp sting of initial loss fades
The dull heavy ache of grief creeps in
While reality and resignation deepen in shades

The pain is not less as time goes by
Rather it changes form with time
Never gone and never less
Merely a different chime

So what response is there to have?
Must sorrow remain and rule?
What hope can be found in this?
Can what is gone find renewal?

Hope only can be found in the Founder of renewal
In the Author and Orchestrator of life
He alone can determine our time and frame
In Him alone is the power and knowledge to control life

Through Him renewal is formed and made
Without Him is only corruption of all
In this life and after in eternity
In Him does all goodness fall

*In Him is the only hope of salvation
From Him alone comes our source of strength
He is the only certainty in this life
He is the only one for whom time has no length*

*Why does my soul despair?
Why is it distraught?
Hope in the Lord, whom I will praise.
He is my help and my God.*

Evelyn Bray

Appendix A:
Is Faith Enough?[viii]

So many people have become frustrated, discouraged, and even walked away from God, because they had prayed for something that never happened; someone to be saved, changed, healed, etc. The philosophy that our faith is directly correlated to our prosperity, health or success is becoming increasingly popular, but is not biblically founded. The Bible does say that if we have faith we can move mountains, but it also says that we will face hardship. The Bible says that if we ask with faith that it will happen, but it also says that we need to delight in God before we get what we want. There are a few key points from the Bible that we need to analyze about our faith before we give way to discouragement and doubt:

1- <u>Is your faith really *faith*</u>? If you believe that God could do it, but don't believe that He will, you are believing in God's ability, but not trusting in His love and good will. Genuine faith is believing what God says in the Bible, acting on it, and leaving the result to God, believing in God not the outcome. If you try to make it happen on your own, or worry about whether/how it will happen, you are not exercising faith. Worry erases the prayer that you just prayed because it shows that you don't trust God. You need to have faith in Him and nothing else, and that comes through in prayer. "Now faith is the assurance of things hoped for, the conviction of things not seen." Hebrews 11:1

2- <u>Are your motives pure?</u> Why do you want what you are praying for? Is it for yourself or someone else? Maybe what you want is a good thing, even something that God says should happen, your husband becoming the spiritual leader of your home for example. But if you want it so that it will make things better for you, your motives are not pure. Selfish motives will not produce anything good. The Bible says that we are supposed to serve others, to love them more than ourselves and put their best interests first and that should be evident in our prayer lives as well. We need to put their interests and good before our own. "You ask and do not receive, because you ask with wrong motives, so that you may spend it on your pleasures." James 4:3

3- <u>Is your request really God's will?</u> Maybe you are praying for healing for someone, which is a good thing to want, but it may not be God's will for them to be healed. He may have some purpose, some good thing that will come through their illness, maybe a person they can reach out to through that suffering, or something to teach them that they would never learn in health. Sometimes what we ask God to do is really our responsibility to do. Maybe you are asking God to heal a sickness, but what God really wants is for you to seek medical help. It does not mean that God is not working if you are healed through medicine. It's just a different avenue. Maybe there was someone at the doctor's office that He wanted you to reach out to that you would never have met otherwise. Maybe you are asking God for self control to quit an addiction, but God wants you to step out and *exert* self control, rather than expecting Him to do it for you. We also need to look at what God has actually promised. He never said we wouldn't suffer. We should pray more for courage and strength to endure suffering than for relief from it. We can also ask Him to give us the right motives. "Because of the surpassing greatness of the revelations, for this reason, to keep me from exalting myself, there was given me a thorn in the flesh, a messenger of Satan to torment me—to keep me from exalting myself! Concerning this I implored the Lord three times that it might leave me. And He has said to me, "My grace is sufficient for you, for power is perfected in weakness." Most gladly, therefore, I will rather boast about my weaknesses, so that the power of Christ may dwell in me. Therefore I am well content with weaknesses, with insults, with distresses, with persecutions, with difficulties, for Christ's sake; for when I am weak, then I am strong." 2 Corinthians 12:7-10. It was not God's will for Paul to be relieved of the thorn in his flesh, even though Paul had faith. God's will was for Paul to stay humble.

4- <u>Is the time really right?</u> Maybe it is God's will for someone to be healed, but not right now. In Acts 3:1-16, Peter and John healed a lame man. But that man had been there, at that very place, while Jesus was on earth, and Jesus never healed him. It just wasn't the right time. For whatever reason, he had to wait to be healed until after Jesus' death. Remember how many in the Bible were promised something by God, but had to wait years before they came true. Abraham was promised a son, but had to wait 25 years for that promise to be fulfilled, until he was 100 and beyond any physical hope.

5- <u>Are you seeing the big picture?</u> What happens is not always "about us." This goes along with #3. Maybe this trouble *is* God's will for you. There are some things that you can only learn in the storm. Are you listening for what God has to teach you, or only for what you want to hear? Remember when Jesus walked on water. The disciples were afraid because of the storm, but as long as Peter focused on Jesus, he could walk on water. As soon as he focused on the storm, he sank. He didn't care about the storm he was in as long as he had the right focus. "But we have this treasure in earthen vessels, so that the surpassing greatness of the power will be of God and not from ourselves; we are afflicted in every way, but not crushed; perplexed, but not despairing; persecuted, but not forsaken; struck down, but not destroyed; always carrying about in the body the dying of Jesus, *so that the life of Jesus also may be manifested in our body. For we who live are constantly being delivered over to death for Jesus' sake, so that the life of Jesus also may be manifested in our mortal flesh."* 2 Corinthians 4:7-11 (emphasis added). This is the big picture, this is the purpose!

6- <u>Is your God still worthy of your trust?</u> Look at God's power, knowledge, love, faithfulness, justice, mercy. Is there anything bad or unworthy in Him? Remember, life is not about you, it is about God. "Whether, then, you eat or drink or whatever you do, do all to the glory of God." 1 Corinthians 10:31. Our motive in everything we do should be God. His will and purposes come first. And whether we acknowledge it or not, that is how it will happen. We can either work toward that or against it. Is He worth trusting?

Remember, when you do not understand the WAYS of God, rely on the CHARACTER of God.

Psalm 22:5

To You they cried out and were delivered;
In You they trusted and were not disappointed.

Appendix B:
Why is There Suffering?

Why do we suffer? Why am I going through this? Why is life so hard? Why do the innocent seem to pay for the crimes of the wicked? Why did God allow this to happen?... We have all asked at least one of these questions at some time, and for many it is the reason why faith in God is ultimately rejected. The idea that a loving, all-powerful God would allow such horrible tragedies is reprehensible to our way of thinking. Unfortunately, many stop at the questions and never get an answer.

> **Genesis 3:17-19 New American Standard Bible (NASB)**
> Then to Adam He said, "Because you have listened to the voice of your wife, and have eaten from the tree about which I commanded you, saying, 'You shall not eat from it';
> Cursed is the ground because of you;
> In toil you will eat of it
> All the days of your life.
> "Both thorns and thistles it shall grow for you;
> And you will eat the plants of the field;
> By the sweat of your face
> You will eat bread,
> Till you return to the ground,
> Because from it you were taken;
> For you are dust,
> And to dust you shall return."

The ultimate reason there is suffering in the world is because of sin. Sin is disobedience: anything we do that is contrary to God's ways or commands. In a sense, it is spiritual treason because it is choosing to follow God's enemy, satan, rather than God.

God did not create sin. He created a perfect, beautiful world without death, disease, suffering, pain or anything bad. It was without fault, and mankind was blessed to live in that perfection as perfect beings in perfect union with God. But then mankind sinned. Adam and Eve chose to rebel against God and paid the consequences for it. Yet, those consequences did not affect them only, but all of humanity and all of creation as well. Sin literally cursed the very ground they walked on.

While sin is the cause of all suffering, there are three main categories of sin that cause us to suffer:
1. The first is our own sin. We do something wrong and suffer the consequences of it. When we lie or steal, we suffer the consequences of not being trusted (not to mention any legal ramifications that may arise.)
2. The second is others' sin. We suffer because of the choices others make, especially in the family unit. Children suffer because of the choices of their parents and vice versa. Sometimes we suffer due to the choices of the government or those in authority. We are connected with others so in some way what we do affects them and what they do affects us.
3. The third is the result sin has on this world. God did not make the world to have storms, disease, cancer, genetic mutations, sickness or natural disasters. It was perfect, but sin corrupted it. Weeds and thorns grow among crops. Storms come to damage the earth. Genes mutate to cause problems and disabilities. Sickness, disease and cancer plague our bodies. These are signs that we live in a fallen world which is longing for God to redeem and restore it.

Hebrews 12:4-11 New American Standard Bible (NASB)
You have not yet resisted to the point of shedding blood in your striving against sin; and you have forgotten the exhortation which is addressed to you as sons,
"MY SON, DO NOT REGARD LIGHTLY THE DISCIPLINE OF THE LORD,
NOR FAINT WHEN YOU ARE REPROVED BY HIM;
FOR THOSE WHOM THE LORD LOVES HE DISCIPLINES,
AND HE SCOURGES EVERY SON WHOM HE RECEIVES."
It is for discipline that you endure; God deals with you as with sons; for what son is there whom *his* father does not

discipline? But if you are without discipline, of which all have become partakers, then you are illegitimate children and not sons. Furthermore, we had earthly fathers to discipline us, and we respected them; shall we not much rather be subject to the Father of spirits, and live? For they disciplined us for a short time as seemed best to them, but He *disciplines us* for *our* good, so that we may share His holiness. All discipline for the moment seems not to be joyful, but sorrowful; yet to those who have been trained by it, afterwards it yields the peaceful fruit of righteousness.

Why does God allow us to suffer the consequences of our own sin?
Consequences are part of the natural course of life. Everything we do has consequences—good for good and bad for bad. We **choose** what we do so we must accept the consequences that come with our choices and actions. If there were no consequences, we would have no reason to do what is right or to avoid what is wrong. It teaches us how to behave.

For those who believe in God we also experience His discipline, like any loving parent disciplines their child. As these verses say, correction is painful in the moment, but if we are trained by it, it yields peace and righteousness.

We also choose our response to suffering and discipline. We can surrender to God and allow Him to use it to grow us and make us more holy like Him, or we can whine and wallow in self pity which will leave us bitter and unhappy without changing our circumstances at all.

Why do the innocent suffer?
Most rebel at the idea of suffering because they feel they do not deserve it. When children suffer at the hands of others it seems especially tragic because we view them as being innocent and undeserving. But are they really?

> **Romans 3:10,23 New American Standard Bible (NASB)**
> as it is written,

> THERE IS NONE RIGHTEOUS, NOT EVEN ONE;...
> for all have sinned and fall short of the glory of God,
> **Psalm 51:5 New American Standard Bible (NASB)**
> Behold, I was brought forth in iniquity,
> And in sin my mother conceived me.

Because of Adam's sin, all are born and conceived in sin. We begin life with a sin nature. The idea that all people are basically good is neither biblical, nor accurate. Roman philosopher Marcus Aurelius said that children are innocent, not because of their nature, but because of their limbs; withhold something from them and they would kill you if they could. Children do not have to be taught to lie, steal or be unkind. They do, however, have to be taught to share, to be obedient, and to be kind. Rather than innocence, it is more a matter of being unable to defend themselves against the choices of those around them. None of us are innocent before God, but we are, or can be, innocent with regard to earthly relationships and circumstances.*

Our view of being innocent or undeserving of punishment is distorted because our view of sin is distorted. If we saw sin as something completely abhorrent and vile, as treason against our holy and perfect God, we would not be surprised that we suffer so much, but instead wonder why we suffer so little. We deserve so much worse than we get because of our rebellion against the holy God. Yet God is merciful and gracious. He does not punish us as we deserve, but allows us to experience only what will bring us to Him in repentance. We deserve to die the moment we commit our first sin, but because God is gracious and merciful, we don't. Instead, He allows us to experience consequences that teach us to not sin.

> **Romans 8:28 New American Standard Bible 1995**
> And we know that God causes all things to work together for good to those who love God, to those who are called according to *His* purpose.
> **2 Corinthians 1:5-7 New American Standard Bible 1995**
> For just as the sufferings of Christ are ours in abundance, so also our comfort is abundant through Christ. But if we are afflicted, it is for your comfort and salvation; or if we are

comforted, it is for your comfort, which is effective in the patient enduring of the same sufferings which we also suffer; and our hope for you is firmly grounded, knowing that as you are sharers of our sufferings, so also you are *sharers* of our comfort.

2 Corinthians 7:8-10 New American Standard Bible 1995
For though I caused you sorrow by my letter, I do not regret it; though I did regret it—*for* I see that that letter caused you sorrow, though only for a while— I now rejoice, not that you were made sorrowful, but that you were made sorrowful to *the point of* repentance; for you were made sorrowful according to *the will of* God, so that you might not suffer loss in anything through us. For the sorrow that is according to *the will of* God produces a repentance without regret, *leading* to salvation, but the sorrow of the world produces death.

This does not mean that we deserve everything bad that happens to us. As His children, God wants us to enjoy good things. Instances of unjust suffering, abuse and loss are devastating and not part of God's original plan for us.

God does not *cause* bad things to happen to us. He gives us free will to make our own choices, and to receive the consequences of those choices. He does not desire for us to suffer, but He also does not want us to sin. He does protect us from some things, but not from everything, allowing what will help us to grow if we trust in Him.

Why does God send people to hell?
He doesn't. It is a choice we make ourselves. Heaven is spending eternity enveloped in God's presence. Would anyone who hates God enjoy that? Why would He force someone who has rejected Him and wants nothing to do with Him, to then spend eternity with Him? He allows us to decide where we will spend eternity. We must accept the results of our choices. But that is not the end...

None of us deserve to go to Heaven. We get so much better than we deserve because of God's grace and mercy. Grace is receiving a gift we don't deserve, and mercy is not receiving the punishment we do deserve. God is just, all sin must be paid for, but we do not always foot the bill.

The greatest story of the innocent suffering unjustly is Jesus Christ, the Son of God. He came to earth, lived a perfect, sinless life, and yet He took on the punishment for the sins of the world. He did not deserve to suffer in any way, yet He suffered cruelly. Why did He suffer? Because He loves us. Our sins, even just one, permanently separate us from God. He is holy and perfect and cannot be in the presence of sin, which means that we are eternally separated from Him. But He loves us so much that He made a way for us to be with Him through the sacrifice of His perfect Son. Jesus paid the debt we owe so that we could live with Him forever!

> **2 Corinthians 5:21 New American Standard Bible (NASB)**
> He made Him who knew no sin *to be* sin on our behalf, so that we might become the righteousness of God in Him.
> **John 3:16-17 New American Standard Bible (NASB)**
> (emphasis added)
> For God so loved the world, that He gave His only begotten Son, that whoever believes in Him shall not perish, but have eternal life. *For God did not send the Son into the world to judge the world, but that the world might be saved through Him.*

It is a common practice with livestock that when a mother loses her baby, the hide of her dead baby is cut off and tied over the back of an orphan in order to get her to adopt it. In this way, when the mother sniffs the orphan she smells her baby and allows it to nurse, accepting it as her own. In the same way, Christ, the only Son of God, died so that His righteous blood could cover us. Then, when God looks at us He sees His Son and accepts us. We just have to accept His sacrifice, **allowing** His blood to cover us and make us right with God. It does not happen to everyone automatically. We have to **choose** it.

What is your choice? Have you accepted Jesus' sacrifice for your sins, surrendering your life to Him? If you have, praise God! Choose to see suffering as God's tool to refine and mold you into His likeness, removing the sinful tendencies that are in you.

If you have not accepted Him, will you now? Repent of your sin and accept His sacrifice for it. Give your life to Him so that you can be righteous before God, He can make you holy and redeem your suffering.

*While we are born and conceived sinful humans, I do not believe that God would send to hell a baby or young child who is too young to understand the concept of salvation. I believe we choose where we go, and if a child is incapable of understanding or making that choice, it would not be just to condemn them. God is always perfectly just. He does not, cannot, do anything wrong or unjust. In 2 Samuel 12:22-23 David said, *"While the child was still alive, I fasted and wept; for I said, 'Who knows, the Lord may be gracious to me, that the child may live.' But now he has died; why should I fast? Can I bring him back again? I will go to him, but he will not return to me."* The Bible does not directly address this issue, but based on God's character and the quote by David stating that he would see his infant child after it died, I believe that those unable to make that choice will not be held responsible for what they are incapable of understanding. At what age a child is able to understand is not definitive, I believe it is different for everyone and only God knows, but we can trust that He will do what is right and just.

Notes

God's Comfort in Suffering
[i] Randy Alcorn, <u>If God is Good</u> (Colorado Springs: Multnomah, 2009) 4.
[ii] <u>Anne of Green Gables</u>. Dir. Kevin Sullivan. Perf. Megan Follows and Colleen Dewhurst. Sullivan, 1985.
[iii] Andrae Crouch. "Soon and Very Soon."

God's Sovereignty over Suffering
[iv] Jerry Bridges, <u>Trusting God</u> (NavPress, 2014) 29.
[v] Brent Curtis and John Eldredge, <u>The Sacred Romance</u> (Nashville: Thomas Nelson, 1997) 159-176.

Our Response to Suffering
[vi] John Wesley, <u>How to Pray</u> (Barbour, 2007) 4.

Stories of Suffering
[vii] Horatio G. Spafford. "It is Well with My Soul." 1873.

Appendix A
[viii] Taken partly from notes on a sermon given by Al Hultein.

The ideas in this book were also greatly influenced by the following books, which I would highly recommend to anyone:

- <u>Trusting God</u> by Jerry Bridges
- <u>Transforming Grace</u> by Jerry Bridges
- <u>Lord Heal My Hurts</u> by Kay Arthur
- <u>A Step Further</u> by Joni Erickson & Steve Estes